UNDERSTANDING
RITA DOVE

Understanding Contemporary American Literature
Matthew J. Bruccoli, Series Editor

Volumes on

Edward Albee • Sherman Alexie • Nicholson Baker
John Barth • Donald Barthelme
The Beats • The Black Mountain Poets • Robert Bly
Raymond Carver • Fred Chappell • Chicano Literature
Contemporary American Drama
Contemporary American Horror Fiction
Contemporary American Literary Theory
Contemporary American Science Fiction, 1926–1970
Contemporary American Science Fiction, 1970–2000
Contemporary Chicana Literature
Robert Coover • James Dickey • E. L. Doctorow • Rita Dove
John Gardner • George Garrett • John Hawkes • Joseph Heller
Lillian Hellman • Beth Henley • John Irving
Randall Jarrell • Charles Johnson • Adrienne Kennedy
William Kennedy • Jack Kerouac • Ursula K. Le Guin
Denise Levertov • Bernard Malamud
Bobbie Ann Mason • Jill McCorkle • Carson McCullers
W. S. Merwin • Arthur Miller • Toni Morrison's Fiction
Vladimir Nabokov • Gloria Naylor • Joyce Carol Oates
Tim O'Brien • Flannery O'Connor • Cynthia Ozick
Walker Percy • Katherine Anne Porter • Richard Powers
Reynolds Price • Annie Proulx • Thomas Pynchon
Theodore Roethke • Philip Roth • May Sarton • Hubert Selby, Jr.
Mary Lee Settle • Neil Simon • Isaac Bashevis Singer
Jane Smiley • Gary Snyder • William Stafford
Anne Tyler • Kurt Vonnegut • David Foster Wallace
Robert Penn Warren • James Welch • Eudora Welty
Tennessee Williams • August Wilson

UNDERSTANDING
RITA
DOVE

Pat Righelato

University of South Carolina Press

© 2006 University of South Carolina

Published in Columbia, South Carolina,
by the University of South Carolina Press

www.sc.edu/uscpress

Manufactured in the United States of America

13   12   11   10   09   08   07   06   8   7   6   5   4   3   2   1

Library of Congress Cataloging-in-Publication Data

Righelato, Pat, 1944–
    Understanding Rita Dove / Pat Righelato.
        p. cm. — (Understanding contemporary American literature)
    Includes bibliographical references and index.
    ISBN-13: 978-1-57003-637-8 (cloth : alk. paper)
    ISBN-10: 1-57003-637-3 (cloth : alk. paper)
    1. Dove, Rita—Criticism and interpretation. 2. Women and
literature—United States—History—20th century. 3. African
Americans in literature. I. Title. II. Series.
    PS3554.O884Z85 2006
    813'.54—dc22

                                              2006005142

for Renton, Sarah, and Rachel
and
Hannah

Contents

Series Editor's Preface

The volumes of *Understanding Contemporary American Literature* have been planned as guides or companions for students as well as good nonacademic readers. The editor and publisher perceive a need for these volumes because much of the influential contemporary literature makes special demands. Uninitiated readers encounter difficulty in approaching works that depart from the traditional forms and techniques of prose and poetry. Literature relies on conventions, but the conventions keep evolving; new writers form their own conventions—which in time may become familiar. Put simply, *UCAL* provides instruction in how to read certain contemporary writers—identifying and explicating their material, themes, use of language, point of view, structures, symbolism, and responses to experience.

The word *understanding* in the titles was deliberately chosen. Many willing readers lack an adequate understanding of how contemporary literature works; that is, what the author is attempting to express and the means by which it is conveyed. Although the criticism and analysis in the series have been aimed at a level of general accessibility, these introductory volumes are meant to be applied in conjunction with the works they cover. They do not provide a substitute for the works and authors they introduce, but rather prepare the reader for more profitable literary experiences.

M. J. B.

Acknowledgments

I wish to thank Rita Dove for the inspiration of her poetry and for the generous permission she has given me to quote from her work. I would also like to thank her husband, Fred Viebahn, for permission to reproduce the photo of Rita on the dust jacket of the book. I am indebted to the School of English and American Literature in the University of Reading, U.K., for granting research leave to enable me to complete the project. Colleagues Ron Knowles, Geoffrey Harvey, Lionel Kelly, Peter Stoneley, and Grace Ioppolo read parts of the typescript and gave help and encouragement. I am very grateful to them. Carole Robb, the school secretary, and her staff provided an efficient and sympathetic working environment. Students of American poetry courses have been enthusiastic co-readers and critics of Dove's writing. I am indebted also to Barbara and Simon Salisbury for sharing their musical knowledge with me when I was working on poems with musical themes.

UNDERSTANDING
RITA DOVE

CHAPTER 1

Introduction

Rita Dove, Pulitzer Prize winner, former poet laureate of the United States, is a writer who has always avoided categorization, opening doors between otherwise distinct artistic spaces. Indeed, one of the ways she comes to mind is in a doorway, securely in the old neighborhood, in family, in the local and specific. Yet she has, from the beginning, stepped through doorways, tested herself, and explored what is beyond as an international poet at home in symposia in Berlin, Brazil, Israel, and South Africa, a much-traveled cosmopolitan figure welcomed and admired in many countries.

As an American poet, Dove has negotiated her artistic space with grace and determination. Like an athlete, she has seen herself as in for the long haul, not looking for supportive habitats in either black or feminist conclaves but shaking off parochialism by living and writing in Europe, connecting, in the volume *Museum* (1983), for example, the lives of black Americans, European medieval saints, colonial adventurers, and that of her own father. *Museum* was followed by *Thomas and Beulah* (1986), a poem sequence of considerable formal originality in which she inserted the particulars of her grandparents' lives into American history. In *Mother Love* (1995), European classical mythology is fused with contemporary American culture. *On the Bus with Rosa Parks* (1999) not only focuses on the achievement of ordinary women in the American civil rights movement but also, in "The Venus of Willendorf," wittily links European artistic creativity with ethnicity and sexuality.

These have been tough and intricate projects, but just as the title of her most recent volume, *American Smooth* (2004), refers to a form of ballroom dancing that permits individual improvisation and virtuosity, so the artistic execution has been fluent and accomplished. Dove is a major writer in the canon of American poetry, standing comparison with preceding established figures such as Wallace Stevens, Marianne Moore, Langston Hughes, and Robert Lowell, as well as her contemporary, John Ashbery. It might seem surprising to link her most closely with Lowell and Ashbery, but she is like them in that her poetry is, in its entirety, a critique of American culture: like Lowell, she reveals history through the prism of the family; like Ashbery, fascinated by the materiality of the painted canvas, she accepts materialist culture as the medium of contemporary existence. Like both, she seeks new ways in which to express the autobiographical.

Each chapter of this book focuses on a single volume of poetry as an artistic entity, analyzing the crosscurrents—stylistic, formal, thematic, and cultural—that give each collection its distinctive quality. Some of the volumes, such as *Thomas and Beulah* and *Mother Love,* are obviously composed as a narrative and symbolic unity. In contrast, the first major collection, *The Yellow House on the Corner* (1980), is made up of more disparate elements. Nevertheless, it releases, shapes, and sets in train the motifs—mythical, historical, familial, and autobiographical— that become the poet's artistic capital.

As part of the exploration of the way in which a volume works on the reader, I have given detailed consideration to individual poems. My readings are intended as provisional, so that other readers can move in and find their own way, responding, resisting, ready to think about how this poetry was produced and to consider specific critical approaches. To this end, I have touched on issues of cultural context and history as starting points for discussion and deployed critical approaches such as gender and reader-response as preliminary rather than exhaustive theoretical demonstrations. Information or explanation has, at times, been given in the text, rather than as notes, in order to draw attention to the poet's range of reference and allusion without unnecessary interruption. This, I hope, is in the spirit of Dove's art, to open the door, to leave it ajar, and to keep the poetry itself center stage.

Dove, a musician, an accomplished singer and ballroom dancer, has said that "musical structure affects . . . how the poems are ordered in a book"[1] and that she has a predilection for five sections in structuring a volume. The extent to which each volume is contrapuntal in the placing of individual poems and, overall, symphonic in the relationship of different sections is always significant. The sense of a musical intelligence at work is evident also in the thematic harmonies of a volume. This is apparent in a motif (often itself musical) such as the mandolin or the canary in *Thomas and Beulah,* which has both a formal compositional and a human developmental value. Or it is revealed in the way in which *Museum* plays past against present, European against African American, embellishing and modifying motifs, shifting scale and tempo. The working out of an individual poem is, for Dove, like a "resolution of notes": "The way that a chord will resolve itself, is something that applies to my poems—the way that, if it works, the last line of the poem, or the last word, will resolve something that has been hanging for a while."[2] Two of her collections, *Grace Notes* (1989) and

American Smooth (2004), have musical titles, one a term relating to classical music, the other to ballroom dance. Music is, indeed, the keynote of her poetry; it is the life of her poems about musicians as well as the poems rhythmically animated by blues, jazz, or classical forms.

Dove's musicality has, at its core, an abstract rigor, an acute sense of pattern and proportion: an early poem that made her reputation was titled "Geometry." This spatial imagination is evident in the visual layout of poems with variations in line justification, most notably in *Mother Love,* or in diamond- and cross-shaped poems in the *Cameos* sequence of *On the Bus with Rosa Parks,* or in the elongated inverse triangle shapes of "Twelve Chairs" (poems designed for chair backs) in *American Smooth.* The spatial aspect is also apparent in the placing of poems within a volume. A devotee of crossword puzzles, Dove enjoys leaving clues for the reader to follow, to recognize patterns and numerical play, but she, teasingly, resists the reader's, and perhaps her own, desire for order and completion. Her imagination also expresses that which is not controllable, recognizes in her patterning the throw of the dice, the predicament of the individual netted in the larger patterns of history, as so wittily expressed in "The Sailor in Africa" (*Museum*) or, more poignantly, in the rueful acknowledgment of Thomas, in *Thomas and Beulah,* at the moment of death.

In her locating of the self, the family, and the ethnic and social group within a historical framework, Dove is Robert Lowell's successor, as surely as she is the successor of Langston Hughes and Melvin B. Tolson. She has brought African American history into the mainstream of American poetry. "Not Welcome Here" in *American Smooth,* for example, is a group of poems in journal form written from the perspective of African

American soldiers who fought in Europe in the First World War; the poems recreate their musical expressiveness in the face of not only danger but also racist injustice from the American command. Dove has shown that the seismic cultural shifts of the twentieth century, the great migration of black labor in the early years of the century and the civil rights movement of the mid-century, are significant events of American history, that these struggles of oppressed groups for the rights of freedom and for the pursuit of happiness have shaped the lives of all Americans today.

For all that Dove has taught Americans how to apprehend their own connectedness, it is a sign of her imaginative reach that she feels profound poetic affinity for Austrian poet Rainer Maria Rilke, whose *Sonnets to Orpheus* she acknowledges as an inspiration for *Mother Love,* her variations on the sonnet form. There is also a Rilkean intensity in the condensing of her symbolist poems, mythic, culturally questing, ironic, yet with an ardor tamped in their meticulous craftings. Essentially Rilkean, too, is the sense of room made within the ordinary, as in his poem "The Unicorn," in which people left room for the imagining of a unicorn. Dove, too, from her opening volume, *The Yellow House on the Corner,* has the confidence to leave space in her poetry for the expansions that transform the known.

CHAPTER 2

The Yellow House on the Corner
Disclosures and Connections

The Yellow House on the Corner, Rita Dove's first full-length volume of poetry, was published when she was twenty-eight. At the heart of her enterprise is an exploration of the African American experience of slavery and its cultural meaning for her generation. This historical recovery of the American past is juxtaposed with poems that express her experience of living in Germany in the 1970s, where, as a young black American, she was an object of curiosity. Arriving with the perceptions of a U.S. citizen, she was jolted by the encounter with European ways of suffering and perceiving in the long aftermath of the Second World War. Her openness to history is matched by an intimate sense of the contemporary in the series of poems that portray the hothouse of American teen dreams, adolescence in a consumer society. Travel, as so often for Dove, is central to the volume, not only the poet as tourist but also the imaginative journey, in her words, a "reach back to childhood" or to history or to other cultures that reveals "some disclosure, some *connection* waiting to be seen."[1] In her experiments with form, Dove condenses contemporary experience into mythic intensity, examining how myth shades off into folklore and fairy tale, the potent cultural narratives that inhabit us in childhood, adolescence, and beyond. The narrative strand of her work is, from the outset, in productive tension with a sparer, elliptical lyric impulse that deploys color as symbolic expression.

"This Life"

The poems of *The Yellow House on the Corner* are in five sections or suites. "This Life," the first poem, lays down an opening motif, an exploration of a modern sense of American identity, examining how it can assimilate and come to terms with ways of thinking and feeling in which being an American is irrelevant. What it is like to be a German, a northern European, might seem as strange in relation to American mainstream culture as to live in a black urban ghetto: both are an "alternate universe"[2] to be imagined through their respective mythologies. As a high-achieving Fulbright scholar studying at the University of Tübingen in 1974, Dove was neither a black American ghettoized adolescent nor a traumatized survivor of the war in Europe. Her inhabitings of these worlds are provisional and disorientating, a deliberate shakeup of a comfortable sense of self-possession:

> I realized that during my rather sheltered college years at Miami University, in the rural setting of southwestern Ohio, I had filled the role of the striving, gifted Black student extremely well, but without much concern for the outside world. And now, suddenly, in Germany I was on display in a strange environment where some people pointed with fingers at me and others pitied me as a symbol for centuries of brutality and injustice against Blacks. So I felt simultaneously alienated both from my home country and from the place I was in. On the other hand . . . serious travel can heighten the awareness a writer needs to see many sides of a story.[3]

Having been the object of cultural stereotyping, Dove characteristically moves from the passivity of objectification to an active examination in her art of how myth shapes and accounts for human behavior. She juxtaposes aspects of the two cultures, European and American, in poems that take on the habitation of their respective myths, perceiving them as survival strategies and expressions of spirit, albeit reductive ones, in the face of adversity. As a writer she turns her own estrangement to account.

Travel, however, is also pleasure and the anticipation of pleasure. "This Life" expresses the charge of expectation that strangers bring to one another. For the feminine speaker of the poem, this adult encounter has to be realized in relation to a picture she loved as a child. The Japanese woodcut imprinted a model of gendered behavior, of feminine passivity:

> As a child, I fell in love
> with a Japanese woodcut
> of a girl gazing at the moon.
> I waited with her for her lover.

Thus, when the speaker of the poem meets an intriguing stranger, she realizes that the unseen lover in the woodcut "had / your face, though I didn't know it." Nevertheless, the model of the feminine in the work of art has to be negotiated into the reality of the here and now. There is a moment in the poem when all the possibility of fantasy takes concentrated form, becomes condensed in the man sitting opposite, becomes all the "golden dresses in a nutshell." However, the image of feminine desire realized is one of essence *and* reduction: closing the gap between fantasy and reality so neatly would be a static entrapment like the girl in the work of art. The poet captures both the fantasy and the real-life uncertainty of the outsider in a situation charged with potential intimacy. Feminine susceptibility to the idea of romance as charmed destiny is tested by the actualities of travel. This testing is evident in the shift from the visual to the tactile at the end of the poem: the white and gold dream gives way to the sensory particularity of "the tough skins of figs." However, neither dream nor reality is privileged in the poem; both are recharged by the presence of the other. The unity of a particular life is made up of such connections and transformations.

Dove's response to Europe was not confined to erotic encounter. Her periods of living in Germany and her marriage to a German writer in 1979 gave her an insight into the devastation of German communities in the Second World War, the weight of suffering, the imprisonment and distortion of spirit that war entails. In the poem "The Bird Frau," nature is imaged in metaphors of military combat, the "sun losing altitude over France," whereas the fierce survival strategies of a civilian woman on a starvation diet of determination are portrayed in images of nature. "The Bird Frau," about one woman's preparations for the return of her wounded son, finely balances the crazed joy with the unsentimental ruthlessness with which the woman "fed the parakeet, / broke its neck" to provide for him. The bird imagery is, first, "a whirring curtain of flak," an image of the terrors of combat, then, in the second stanza, it is a food source to be plundered from nature, and finally, it is a celebratory halo around the woman, who, as "an old rag bird," physically wasted, is terrifying to children. Her wildness marks her as ideologically still at war yet as having regressed to an asocial existence: in her deprivations she is closer to the birds than to humans. She has become like a fairy-tale witch. Most poignant is the ambiguity of tenses in the poem: it is uncertain whether her son's return is but a figment of her crazed imagination.

History takes on more symbolist expression in "The Snow King." Its fairy-tale opening, "In a far far land," is at first reassuringly distanced, mythically remote. Yet this mythic realm is the landscape of the holocaust in which the frozen bodies of sparrows are the image of common humanity, those who become victims. Is the snow king the perpetrator of "the lime-filled spaces" in which the whiteness has become the image of mass execution carried out in the name of whiteness, of ethnic purity? Or is he the liberal humanitarian who weeps helplessly and nostalgically yet remains bound up in romantic dreams of the future? The uneasy parameters of the politics of mythic consciousness are rendered in the ambivalent moral status of the snow king. Northern fairy tales shape nationalistic and ethnic consciousness: "fire" and "lime" are not culturally neutral elements; the dead sparrows encumber the purity of vision. The last line, "His cracked heart a slow fire, a garnet" is indicative of the poem's fine ambiguity of symbolic reference: the phrases are perfectly applicable to the natural process of seasonal change, ice cracking in heat, but the "slow fire" and the blood-red "garnet" suggest more sinister cultural distortions and determinations as well as the process that melts the snow and weeps for the ravages of ideological winter. The garnet stone is named after the pomegranate, the Christian symbol of resurrection, and associated with the classical myth of Persephone, who returns to regenerate the earth each spring. The realm of the snow king encompasses all of this: the deeds done in the name of ethnic purity and the thaw, the process of recognition and recovery. The very concise form of the poem and the conjunction of determined distancing and present-tense predicament suggest how cultures carry the burden of their antecedents even as they emphasize their remoteness. The snow king "roams" the historical traces of a season of winter.

It is surely not accidental that "The Snow King" is placed next to "Sightseeing," a laconic view of the collateral damage of the Second World War. German villagers, returning after Allied occupation of their church, leave the broken statues as a symbol of the desecration of their culture. The speaker of the poem considers whether it is possible for the statues to be looked at neutrally, without symbolic enhancement, without an ideological reading. The doubling in the title, "Sightseeing," incorporates the idea of seeing twice, as if different spectators inspect the sight / site from their own ideological perspective. Throughout the poem, the verbs of looking strain for escape from symbolic conferral or search for wiser-than ways of looking, but the language always locks back into ideology, into a symbolic mode. Humanity is constitutionally prone to see sights in signifying ways. The casual sightseer flaunting hindsight does not have any particular premium on objectivity. Living in Germany made Dove aware that the wreckages of war were images it was important to "*regard*" (emphasis added) with the meaning of both "to look again" and "to have a respect for."

The Germany of the first section of the volume consists of small rural communities, narrow, resilient, sometimes cruel survivors of war bound up in an icy and alien mythology. Yet this dour imaginative topography is also the culture of musical genius, of a fecund life-force that is comically rendered in "Robert Schumann, or: Musical Genius Begins with Affliction," as if all those works of his in A are alphabetically aligned to the affliction of art. Schumann, beset with sound, is like a huntsman frenziedly in pursuit of some internal clarion call:

> It never stops: the alarm
> going off in his head is a cry
> in a thicket of its own making.

A is sexual abandonment and libido (Schumann was to father seven children), the Adam in the garden of Eden grasping not just one apple but the sky raining apples, the stacked-up musical works in A, and the outpouring of notes that afflict Schumann in the joyous sense of excess of creative energy, as if music has taken hold of him. He is not yet afflicted in the other sense of the word, as he was to be, in midlife, deteriorating into mental illness and finally death in an asylum. The poem does not dwell on the "wretched sounds," the tragic ending of his life, but expresses the fragile, erotic revel of Schumann's mind in the "thicket" of its own fantasies, teetering between anarchy and control, between solipsistic obsession and creative release that somehow just, just, miraculously, transforms into the musical phrases on the score sheets. Romantic delirium, romantic grandeur and romantic creation—beginning something, "starting over"—is reimagined in an American colloquial diction, an equivalent of Schumann's "naked" enterprise. The poem wittily imitates sexual activity and musical form in its pattern of surge and return, of motif declared, extended, and recovered, the imagery of notes vertiginously stacked up yet returned to A. Creativity is divine irritant, Dionysiac affliction. Dove triumphantly turns around the mythology of Schumann's life: it "*begins* with affliction."

The locus of the last three poems of the first section is the United States, but they are not about being at home in "the old neighborhood" in the comfortable sense of Dove's poem of that title. In an African American idiom, they express contemporary black urban experience of the short fuses of racial tension. "Teach Us to Number Our Days" and "Nigger Song: An Odyssey" empathize with the dreams and delinquent energies of young black males imprisoned in their ill-environed lives. The title quotation of the former, from Psalm 90, is an ironic comment on its injunction against spiritual complacency. The psalm urges that death and last things should not be forgotten in the midst of life's bounties, but the inhabitants of the neighborhood described in the poem are taught to number their blighted days in a different way. The "blue bean" in the fairy tale of Jack and the Beanstalk is transformed from a child's dream of success and escape into a cop's "blue bullet," which will "take root in his gut." A boy from this neighborhood has no chance of escape.

Dove, however, does not regard poetry as the medium for proposing activist solutions to racial problems or for explicit black proselytizing. Her attitude is more oblique. The issue is represented surrealistically in "Upon Meeting Don L. Lee, in a Dream," a poem that, as Ekaterini Georgoudaki has observed, is critical of the black arts movement aesthetic in the seventies of which Lee (now known as Haki R. Madhubuti) was a major representative. Georgoudaki notes that "through a cluster of surrealistic images, she [Dove] suggests the decay of the ideology that Don Lee embodies"[4] when his "hair falls out in clumps" and he is interrupted and cut off by a speaker representative of Dove herself. The myth of Lee disintegrates under the flame-thrower successor who steals his fire. This is a comic feminist putdown of masculine posturing, yet it is also a significant artistic positioning for Dove as a young poet coming up against the established black ideology. In this early poem, Dove is separating herself from the exclusive celebration of blackness, the homophobic and racist polemics that Lee preached. In a later interview, Dove acknowledged it as "a generational poem," saying that at the beginning of her career,

I was terrified that I would be kind of suffocated before I began. That I would be pulled into the whole net of whether I was black enough or whether I was denigrating my own people and all this kind of stuff. This is a pressure, not just from the black arts movement, but this is a pressure of one's whole life, to be a credit to the race.[5]

Nevertheless, Dove is not unsympathetic to the expression of blackness or to black male energy. Her readiness to use proverbial language for the commonplace fears of a black neighborhood in "Teach Us to Number Our Days" is given a different twist in "Nigger Song: An Odyssey," which mimics the stereotype but also expresses the syncopated rhythm of six black youths adventuring into the "gray-green nigger night," the derelict landscape that they "ink" with their energy, in pursuit of danger. Like Odysseus, they are storming the underworld. The poem exults in the mythology of black energy, albeit with the irony that Odysseus returned from the underworld, whereas these modern joy riders live dangerously and embrace extinction.

Back

The second suite includes autobiographical poems that return to an American iconography. In contrast to the bleakness of postwar Europe, America is the land of plenty. This second section is playful and confident, opening with two poems about the art of poetry, "Five Elephants" and "Geometry," the latter immediately recognized by critics as a surge in attainment, a landmark achievement for a young poet, of a kind equivalent to Elizabeth Bishop's "The Map." "Five Elephants," less well known, is also remarkable. The poem is about memory, about wallowing in unhappiness, refusing "consolation." The five elephants that arrive on cue signify the weight of memory. Yet they are also in linked movement and, after some resistance, the speaker turns and follows them. This is a witty figural anecdote about personal emotion and art as well as the potentiality of metaphor. Are the elephants merely to be ponderous carriers of memory? Or are they "clumsy ballerinas," signifying the shape and movement of the poem that comes unexpectedly? The elephants, coming at dawn from the east, cursive, "hooking the sky," release the "frozen / tear in the brain" into creativity. The poem bypasses the confessional mode, opting for art rather than tears. As an anecdote about creativity, it complements "Geometry," the poem on the facing page.

Whereas the elephants remain a physical presence in their poem, "Geometry" is about imaginative release and expansion as a kind of abstract clarification. The parallels and contrasts between proving a theorem in geometry and writing a poem that attains a "point true and unproven" are themselves a succinct exercise, an intellectual pleasure in figuration. As Helen Vendler has shown,[6] the patterning is subtle and allusive, with verbs such as "intersected," appropriate to geometry, but also suggestive of "insect," connecting to "butterflies," symbolic of psyche, the flight of the spirit. Nature and mind are in harmonious abstraction: even the scent of flowers would be an encumbrance to this transparency, the clearing and expansion of space. The transcendence, the sense of open space, takes place *within* the space of the room: the windows have "jerked free," "hinged into butterflies," transformed and expanded yet remain incisively angled. The mind is out in the open because the pattern is clarifying, not because it has left the house. Every image of freedom in the poem is part of an enhancement of given parameters, true to the spirit of geometry as well as of art. The imagery of glass is the intersection of nature and culture and, at the same time, the metamorphosis of one into the other:

> As the walls clear themselves of everything
> but transparency, the scent of carnations
> leaves with them.

These lines are both precisely active and hoveringly ambiguous: "leaves" is a verb of purposeful departure and, if read momentarily as a noun at the turn of the line, suggests that the foliage is somehow distilled into the transparency, part of the essence. The grace and artistry of the three tercets lies in their expressive paradox: abstraction as clarification yet also euphoric liberation, not from nature but of nature. It might be said that Wallace Stevens's great poem of outside/inside, of artistic inception, "Not Ideas about the Thing but the Thing Itself,"[7] finds its counterpart in this poem celebrating the thing made in all its hinges and angles and lightness of being. Poetry is as exact as geometry but with a tensile suspension of meaning.

The long poem in the second section, "Suite for Augustus," is an experiment in form, a rendering of the history of a love affair in an elliptical narrative of linked short poems. Dove perfects this mode in *Thomas and Beulah* and in fine-tuned variations in later volumes (*Cameos,* for example, in *On the Bus with Rosa Parks*). "Suite for Augustus" is expressed autobiographically, as if a diary from the woman's point of view, but it is also more generally representative of black middle-class experience defined by the contemporary cultural landmarks of the era: the poem opens with President Kennedy's death in 1963. It is a modern romance conducted across distances. Augustus reigns imperially in the heart of the feminine speaker who worships him. As a broadcaster, Augustus is beamed by satellite all over the continent, but his ubiquity makes him inaccessible to his lover, left behind alone in bed "stretched out under percale," which comically suggests that her aspirations might be more home-making and domestic than his. In fact, Augustus always seems to be just leaving, particularly if anything familial is in train, packing his bag when the lovers are together in Georgia for July Fourth celebrations.

"D.C.," the second poem in "Suite for Augustus," considers how the city is itself a museum to past presidents, most obviously Washington in the memorabilia, the "brontosaurus bones," including his "wooden dentures," in the Smithsonian and the naming and layout of the city. It is also a relic of the lovers' visit and their shared perceptions. The Washington Monument, for example, which the speaker thinks of as "this outrageous cue stick / lying reflected on a black table," Augustus described as a "bloodless finger." The topography of the monuments reflected in the water is also a map of the city's ethnic composition, the white central power surrounded by the outlying black neighborhoods. The dangerous "no man's land" of the black districts contrasts with the Japanese cherry blossoms picture-postcard image of the civic center of the city. Washington, D.C., is a collection of monuments, a ghost city, in all sorts of ways an improbability for both whites and blacks seeking to find themselves reflected in it. For upwardly mobile black professionals, the city is an opportunity that is not reflected in its topography, the nation-making symbols memorializing white accomplishment.

The final poem, "Back" (the title taken as the header of this section), begins, "Three years too late, I'm scholarshipped / to Europe and back." Too late, that is, to acquire a sophistication to match the urbanity of Augustus, whose international credentials are confirmed by his landing a year later in Kuwait, a political and business opportunity that outshines mere education.

The juxtaposition of divergent destinations is an acknowledgment that the lovers are now separate individuals coming "back" only in memory. Travel has enabled the speaker to emulate Augustus, but even travel seems to have been more passive for the woman, "scholarshipped / to Europe and back," the pun makes her seem like a package. Her thoughts of Augustus on returning to the United States are mingled with the realization that he will not be thinking of her.

In "Suite for Augustus," the individual is linked with the moment of history; furthermore, geography is an image, not only of the racial composition of the United States but also of the couple's pleasure in black identity, not as constraint but as a sensory passport to the world. These two aspiring black professionals have horizons beyond their own country and beyond each other. If Augustus has coincidently been a mentor (and one early meaning of the musical term "suite" was "lesson"), he has no wish to be a Mr. Knightley to her Emma; he is a moving-on man. The suite, in very short compass, traces the first buzz of a relationship and its trajectory, the geographical range an image of the personal developments of two individuals as the relationship changes. Poignantly, the creation of the poems brings the writer back to the moods of the different moments but "led no closer to you." Augustus is elusive still; he has always been on ahead. Yet the affair has been conducted among a Proustian cornucopia of American sixties culture—Kennedy's photo, D.C. monuments, crêpe-paper streamers at high school dances, spare ribs and snow potatoes at a July Fourth barbecue, crème de menthe, cherry blossoms, tubs of ice. The image associations throughout the poems between the political and the personal make a witty parallel between the great public figures coded via their ghostly relics and the sensory ecstasy of an affair also now read as memorabilia.

The suite of poems is an elliptical narrative of the relationship conducted in the modulations between the language of possession and escape, the tension between the woman's fixation, which "reined in each day," and the man's response to the sky as an invitation to departure. The lyric yearning is held and objectified by wry distinctions that give this conventional story a dry contrapuntal urgency in its gender and temporal tensions. These rhythmic disciplines reflect the early associations of the word "suite" in music as meaning a small group of related but sufficiently contrasted compositions with origins in dance and deploying a limited range of motifs. A choice of form that expresses the rhapsody of dance within a limited framework is expressive of the gender roles in this love affair and holds in tension the political and the personal, the immediate and the retrospective vision, the analytic and the lyric voice.

The Underside of History

The poems of the third suite are a sustained effort of historical imagination, all of them an attempt to recover something of the experience of slavery and the efforts in the period of the Revolution and after to change the law. Dove seeks to know and to understand this period of American history, not only to honor the black men and women who figured publicly in antislavery campaigns but also, as she has said, "to reveal the 'underside of history, and to present this underside in discrete moments.'"[8] The poem "The Slave's Critique of Practical Reason" enters the mindset of a slave and ironically adopts the title of Kant's philosophical work of 1788, which concludes that two things fill the mind with awe, the moral law within and the heavens above. The distance between the philosopher and the slave is evident in the latter's more exigent reasons to be practical:

> Ain't got a reason
> to run away—
> leastways not one
> would save my life.
> So I scoop speculation
> into a hopsack.

The vertical layout of the poem and the laconically combined slave idiom with touches of more abstract and figurative language mimes the existence that is both narrowed and genuinely imaginative. Another irony here, perhaps, is that Kant's writing was famously dry and prolix, whereas the slave is witty and succinct, with a drawling turn of the line to the word "leastways" that undermines the initial statement.

The poems about public events, such as "Belinda's Petition," are couched in the ornate diction of the period. The democratic gains of the revolutionary era encouraged blacks to seek freedom, and in 1781 a Massachusetts court interpreted the state's constitution as having abolished slavery. Belinda, the speaker in Dove's poem, refers in her appeal to the revolutionary wars as having severed "the binds of tyranny," thus providing a precedent for her own case. Her speech has a new-found dignity that contrasts with her childhood condition of "Ignorance." The word is capitalized to emphasize the irony that she might now be regarded as unfit for freedom, when what she had been ignorant of as a child was the evil of slave trading, which took away her freedom and enforced her illiteracy:

> How might
> I have known of Men with Faces like the Moon,
> who would ride toward me steadily for twelve Years?

Once the victim of fate in the guise of slave traders, Belinda now actively requests of her newly freed countrymen, "the Same for me": the colloquialism and capitalization breaking through the more polite diction are salient and compelling. The opening of the poem similarly combines solemnity and directness of language to express the unprecedented historical opportunity for Belinda when she addresses "the honorable Senate and House / of Representatives of this country" and then adds at the beginning of the next line "new born," a reminder of their own fledgling state and their newfound chance to give her free birth as opposed to her erstwhile "Existence."

Helen Vendler, in discussing this group of poems, remarks that Dove's "attempts to school herself in black historical memory"[9] have, at this stage of her career, variable poetic dividends. However, I would argue that these poems are as much experiments in narrative form as historical enquiry, and that the two elements are mutually enhancing. The desire to register other ways of feeling, to empathize with an individual consciousness from another time and place, is the cornerstone of Dove's developing poetic strategy. Vendler notes that in these poems, "history has given a prefabricated plot,"[10] but some are more successful than she implies. They are documentary, but the angle of vision can be poignant in an unexpected way. This is the case in "David Walker (1785–1830)," which is, in some respects, a scrupulous exercise in authenticity of historical detail. Walker, an abolitionist so fierce that he alienated even the abolitionist press, was an old-clothes dealer in Boston. The poem juxtaposes the language of his pamphlets and the enraged responses they aroused with a descriptive contextualizing of his world in which pamphlets might be stuffed into "jackets / ringwormed with salt." His militant intransigence is highlighted by the language of "normality" in which his pronouncements are framed, as if the authorities are attempting to contain him: "Free to travel, he still couldn't be shown how lucky / he was." Indeed, the imagery of travel possesses the poem, as an image of the vision that emanates from this shop door, refusing to accept half measures, urging the violent overthrow of white oppressors worldwide. His swelling periods are cut off by his sudden death, his body "found face-down" in his own doorway, "his frame slighter than his friends remembered," a perspective—from the public image of the larger-than-life demagogue to the vulnerable human—that alters our way of seeing him.

"The Transportation of Slaves from Maryland to Mississippi" is equally effective in its historical imagining, perhaps because it focuses on a moment of ideological tension. As Dove writes in her note, a slave woman helps a Negro driver of a wagonload of slaves who have killed two white men and are attempting to escape to remount and ride to his white owner for help. The poem begins with the afterthoughts of the woman slave who pitied and helped the injured Negro driver. This is followed by an official-style report of the incident from a white owner-class perspective that describes how the escaping Negroes are finally "routed." The third section describes the rapidity and brutality of the murder of the two whites. The juxtapositions thus underline competing savageries in which the woman is caught up and that, unwittingly, she becomes the cause of prolonging. The poignancy of the situation of the woman and the injured driver is that they are hardly aware of a conflict of loyalty: their sense of decency and fidelity is aligned to their white owners, not to a desire for freedom.

The most potent poem of the third section is "Cholera," in which cultural ritual, superstition, and sickness are intolerably wrought. A group of slaves, some healthy and some with cholera, have been moved into the woods and fires have been lit, at the doctor's orders, to sweat out the fever. The slaves revert to their own ritual practices to ward off death and to express their spiritual afterlife, dancing round the fire and intoning with a shocking freedom. The doctor, in the face of this, reverts to his own cultural rituals and orders them to be "slicked down with bacon fat and / superstition strapped from them." This does not stop them dancing, as the last line of the poem is the laconic observation, "It was a dance of unusual ferocity." The ravages of the subject are kept in check by the dryness of address that records the episode and is intercut with italicized phrases expressing the delirious imprecations of the dying slaves. The antiphonal mode of different voices with differing kinds of authority is a significant structural feature here, a poetic structure that Dove develops with considerable finesse in *Mother Love* (1995).

These poems are a foray into historical understanding. Dove is not content to be a passive consumer of history but, like Toni Morrison, a writer she admires, seeks to give expression to those who have been without a voice or whose voices have been unfairly mediated. This is also a historicist enterprise, an active shaping of the poet's own modern consciousness to find through these ghostly predecessors a viable contemporary African American identity. The experiments in language are a way of meeting and speaking with the shadowy figures from slave history, these only recently acknowledged guardians of that image-bank of the past, which, as Morrison has said, is one that in many ways Americans do not want to remember.[11] Oral tradition and formal literary decorum are in suspenseful tension in the poems of this section. Sometimes in deliberate incongruous misalliance and sometimes in harmonious counterpoint, the poems enact the process of friction, energy, and accommodation by which a vernacular idiom comes into contact with literary conventions that have evolved from a European tradition of letters. Dove is attentive to the potential of combining oral and written expression: in the very incongruity there is poetry to be made. In such poems, the poet enlarges her own historical consciousness and constructs a method of psychological enquiry that she was to elaborate further in her study of the totalitarian mind in the poem "Parsley" in *Museum* (1983). What is notable, in looking back over this group of poems, is the ambition of the enterprise that feeds into so much of Dove's later work, a continuing, sustained embrace of history as an arena in which language is both given and taken.

Can You Feel It Yet?

The poems of the fourth suite are an immediate contrast to the historical exigencies of slavery. They trace the preoccupations of growing up in contemporary America, and many of them are concerned with the gap between experience and the expectation of experience, or with the anxiously awaited emblems of adolescence. The first three poems, "Adolescence I," "Adolescence II," and "Adolescence III," are favorite anthology pieces. Adolescents look forward, and the question "Can you feel it yet?" encapsulates their anticipations and anxieties. The most successful elements in the series are the comic touches and the opportunities for misreading, as in "Adolescence II," in which a young girl in the bathroom, waiting for the onset of puberty, is interrogated by "three seal men" (cockroaches?): "'Can you feel it yet?' they whisper." The fact that "it" is unspecified is part of the game. The fears and pleasures of sexuality are incipient in the "slice" and "ragged holes" of the "edge of darkness," the sensory distinctions of "fur" and "sleek," "quiver" and "clutch." "Adolescence I" is being told about sex, "Adolescence II" is the cusp of pubescence, and "Adolescence III" is the Freudian displacements of family life and dream of romance with its elaborate rituals of preparation, the battery of effects intended to slay the opposite sex.

This group of poems stays in touch with and registers the ideologies of modern American teen culture. They seem autobiographical only in the most general sense: many women, including women poets, might be reckoned to have had similar experiences. This stance is in itself a postconfessional perspective. It would be difficult to imagine the modernist, Marianne Moore, writing poems on adolescence, and the confessional generation of women poets who followed her, such as Sylvia Plath and Anne Sexton, emphasized the extreme and unusual degree of their own sensations. But Dove's emphasis on the ordinary experience, as in the adolescence poems, extends the range of feminine subject matter, and as experiments they anticipate some of the imagery that becomes richer in Dove's later volumes, such as the "scarred knees" in "Adolescence III" that acquire more complex resonance in the 1989 volume *Grace Notes*.

Other poems in this section rehearse the cultural choices available to women or girls of different cultures. A widowed Indian speaker in "The Kadava Kumbis Devise a Way to Marry for Love" is left in the limbo of choice, finding the arbitrariness of freedom hard to deal with. The poem "Beauty and the Beast" in the fifth section is a fable of the kind of arranged marriage that the widow would have originally made. It seems to suggest that such a marriage could be a secure erotic haven. In contrast,

a young Western woman in "Spy," possibly a prostitute returning from a night's work, finds in the city street a reproachful scenario.

The two poems that complete the section express a more resolute, independent femininity, indeed, a feminist identity, in the
making. "Pearls" and "Nexus" both have an image of an insect
as a visitor from the natural world drawing the speaker's attention away from the problems and egotisms of human relationships. In "Pearls," the freedom of the dragonfly's visit contrasts
with the necklace, "a noose of guileless tears." The lover is a
known, too well known, factor. The circumscribed limits of cou-
pledom contrast with the natural cycle in which at evening "the
sky has nearly forgotten the sun."

However, in the poem "Nexus," to be released from relationship into the claims and disciplines of art is a severe test. Its
seriocomic mode imparts Gothic terrors to the act of writing. A
giant praying mantis (like some grotesque parody of the implor-
ing ghost of Catherine in *Wuthering Heights*), begs for entry at
the window, his "monkey wrench head against the glass." He is
the fear of "formlessness," the urge for expression but the terror of vacancy. But as in Stevens's "Not Ideas about the Thing
but the Thing Itself," the cry from "outside" is like a "sound in
the mind"[12] of the poet. Outside and inside become mutually
enhancing and outside becomes the herald of inner creativity.
Dove's sense of this magic is less portentous than that of Stevens,
but it is equally elated:

> I walked outside;
> the grass hissed at my heels.
> Up ahead in the lapping darkness
> he wobbled, magnified and absurdly green,
> a brontosaurus, a poet.

The giant praying mantis is a "brontosaurus" in that he is like a dinosaurian reptile and because in the etymology of the word, the first part comes from the Greek meaning the noise of thunder, whereas the second part is reminiscent of "thesaurus" (knowledge or word store). Thus, as a "poet," he is both screech and resource of language. He is nature, demanding expression, and, as the famous image of the "begging" apparition at the window reminds us, "bronto" puns on Brontë, the author of *Wuthering Heights*. The "Nexus" of the poem's title is thus a play on the associative links, intertextual and natural, which assail the imagination under the stress of writing. *Wuthering Heights* is itself a novel obsessed with inside/outside and nature/culture relationships and the question of whether these antitheses can be breeched. In Dove's poem, the links between precursor text, nature, poet, and the act of writing are inscribed with a dreamlike compulsion (in the novel, Lockwood has been reading Catherine's journal when she appears at the window in a dream). The danger of "opening onto formlessness" is averted; the poem is created. The poet writes inside; the mantis prays outside. Afterward, the poet walks outside: the mantis, now a brontosaurus, is acknowledged for his share in the process. The last line has an appropriate ambivalence in that the praying mantis as figurative resource is himself dubbed a poet: the word is equally appropriate to the writer, now "outside" the completed poem, the nexus of their relationship.

The group of quasi-autobiographical poems of adolescence and early adulthood of section four, relationship poems as they might be called, lead into the hallucinatory assurance of the last poem. "Nexus" subsumes erotic fantasy into artistic creativity as if the sensual turmoil we suffer can become, if not exactly a contemplative green thought in a green shade, then "absurdly green" in the creative sense, a magnified brim of potentiality on which susceptibility and stubbornness can work.

Lemon-Yellow Nexus

The fifth suite, international, historical, familial, and domestic by turns, has an easy pleasure in its own sensual and sensory diversity. The imagination as a transformational nexus is buoyant. The senses of color and taste connect the exotic and the local, the birds and lemons in the desert and the yellow neighborhood house. The heightened awareness of the whole section, the sense of magical transformations, of revelatory salience, is because these poems seem *shared*. They are all, in a sense, love poems. The first poem, "Notes from a Tunisian Journal," is a revel in sensual transitions: sight becomes perfumed taste in the "nutmeg stick of a boy," becomes tart crunch in the salt stars. "The Sahara Bus Trip" is a more extended humorous narrative of the pleasures and pains of tourism, but this poem, too, has it color ecstasies that even that conventional irritant, the "English tourist" with his "wide-angled lens," cannot despoil. The poem acknowledges the parasitical nature of tourist activity: the blankness of the desert is punctuated by the tourist hotel with its "green interference of palms," but the element of cultural critique is entirely subservient to the couple's shared erotic delight. There is a pleasure in the ordinary/extraordinary quality of the experience reminiscent of Elizabeth Bishop's writing. However, the abiding sentiments are not those of marginality or homelessness: the poem is not really exercised by "questions of travel"[13] but expresses the "tangy" intimacy of love, the sense of a new landscape as an erotic region. Erotic play is also the keynote of "His Shirt," modernist in its sliding of the title into the first line and sentence of the poem, its vertical form and two-line stanzas, and its short line enjambment, reminiscent of William Carlos Williams. Rather than the syncopated rhythms of a Langston Hughes's kind of delivery of a vertical format, the poem unfolds with a more measured, more ostensive deliberation in which the position of each word slows and defers the climax, a form of poetic foreplay appropriate to a love poem.

The concluding poems of the section and of the volume shape up the sense of America as origin and transit camp that, from an internationalized perspective, not only signifies roots yet also exerts a more transformative allure. It is as if the poems return to America to question whether America can provide artistic space. The title, *The Yellow House on the Corner,* suggests that, notwithstanding the foray abroad, the volume intends to remain in touch with origins.

The most significant poem of the volume in its expression of American history and origins is a surprising one. "Corduroy Road" is a reimagining of the pioneering ethos that opened up America, a necessary antidote to the contemporary sense that the jet engine has smoothed the traveler's path to an anodyne degree. A corduroy road, a term from the 1830s, the expansionist era of clearing land and hacking out trails, is a road made of logs laid transversely across swampy ground. The *"Instruction"* in the italicized second stanza of the poem is to clear a track all the way across the state of Wisconsin from west to east, *"From Prairie du Chien to Fort Howard at Green Bay."* The stanzas alternate between the quasi-documentary italicized official language of instruction with its tabulation of casualties and the perspective of a logger on the road felling the forests. The workmen make up games, finding faces in the axe marks on trunks. In the fifth and final stanza, the logger's perspective becomes more reflective:

Whenever a tree is felled, I think of a thousand blankets
ripped into sparks, or that the stillness itself
has been found and torn open with bare hands.

He feels that the "hazard" of the tree felling seems like "contrition" for the despoliation of an environment so rich and so freely available, "wild honey / blazing from outstretched palms." However, the ambiguity of "blazing" as both flamelike color and the act of defacing trees (which ironically, have been razed to look like faces) is finely balanced *between* intensities of natural abundance and human energy and determination. Similarly, tree felling is both a wound and an act of liberation, a "thousand blankets ripped into sparks," as if this dark, dense forest has been opened up by a Promethean energy. That road making has its giddy intensities is evident in the powerful verbs of stanza one: as the tree comes down, the sky "lurched into view"—a space for air to "swoop down."

"Corduroy Road" is a key poem in working out a mode for historical inquiry. It is an important breakthrough in formal terms in that an antiphonal patterning of different kinds of language, the officially distanced and the sensory immediate, is juxtaposed. It allows not only for a pointed contrast between formal documents and individual sensation but also for considerable complexity of understanding. The explicit ecological concerns of the poem underline the necessity of mediating the laborer's sensations in the language of hindsight. Thus in the final stanza, the language has both a physical primacy and, in a phrase such as "What prevails a man to hazard his person in the Wisconsin Forests," a recognition of its own separation from that primacy, its own stiffness and distance from "a skunk bagged." If stanzas 1 to 4 work by antiphonal alternation of voices, the written and the unwritten record (both imaginatively registered or recovered), the fifth stanza admits the language of sensation and thought, intensifying and expanding the exchanges of significance beyond a particular historical era. Thus "contrition" becomes "closer" to the twentieth-century (or twenty-first-century) reader who attributes an emotion, gives a human face to a nineteenth-century statistic in the making of America, and, in doing so, acknowledges that the historicist imagination is not neutral but carries its own ideological baggage, carves its own crude symbolic markings. The "I" of the final stanza is as pertinent to the modern poet or reader as to the nineteenth-century logger or recording clerk, and the ambiguity is a recognition of the complexity of their historical relationships, the symbiotic energies that constitute progress, the razing and opening up that enable the luxury of retrospective editing and imposition of significance. But the poem is not weighed down with this understanding: it is artistically, not polemically, expressed. The last three lines are poignant and powerful:

> What prevails a man to hazard his person in the Wisconsin
>   Forests
> is closer to contrition than anything: the wild honey
> blazing from outstretched palms, a skunk bagged and eaten
>   in tears.

The imagery is of Edenic abundance and desperate survival, human wonder and pain stretching toward us from that outsetting time.

The last poem of the volume is "Ö," the Swedish word for island and an international expression of wonder. It is not surprising that this poem supplies the title phrase for *The Yellow*

House on the Corner. Translation from one language to another carries the same elations as the transformations of metaphor:

> One word of Swedish has changed the whole neighborhood.
> When I look up, the yellow house on the corner
> is a galleon stranded in flowers.

Neighborhood rootedness has the capacity to transform, via the archaism of "galleon," into historical voyaging. The effect is to render both the known and the unknown strange in the incongruity of the "galleon stranded in flowers." The foreign language has the enchanting capacity to make everything foreign. The language is exact in the use of "stranded" as if on the strand or beach, and also with the meaning of left behind, but to be left behind in a garden of flowers would be a pleasing predicament, a surprising joy. As with the windows in the poem "Geometry," the intersection is also an expansive liberation, a kind of aerial delight.

The pleasure is in moving across boundaries of culture and history, in connecting two inert terms to vivify both so that "nothing's / like it used to be, not even the future"; "island" becomes not so much insular as an eager sniffing of the salt sea, "enisled"[14] not in the tremulous Arnoldian sense of separation, but a youthful revel in suspension and flux. The imagination is not becalmed by the contemporary suburban sound of a "leaf-mulcher"; it "could be the horn-blast from a ship," a romantic call to metaphor. The ship lands in the backyard; the house takes off. It is a fantasy quite at home with itself, not straining for exotic vocabulary, indeed, often down-to-earth in idiom.

In a volume much concerned with self-development through the formative effects of travel and with historical recovery and indebtedness, this closing poem celebrates language's transformative journey into the unknown. Dove has found a mode of artistic exploration that is exacting: "Shape" is the first word of the poem, yet this injunction is also "a word . . . found so right it trembles." Precision does not mean fixity or a refusal to "budge" but the delicate active potency of the word, its transformational latency. Like Ariel, the spirit of poetry is airborne. The enjambments of the poem turn the "corner" into new vistas, the lines coming not to an end but as if to a point of departure and change. In this poem about the art of poetry, the title letter turns out to be a word that turns into a poem: the process of poem making is initially a lucky chance, then an act of creative energy in which the reader is imperatively invited to participate, and then, at the end, the deliberately flattened matter-of-fact language reports the completed result: "You start out with one thing, end / up with another."

The mystery of language as translation and transformation, as a talisman to cross boundaries or to metamorphose perception, to create a nexus or constellation of imagery is the imaginative discovery of this volume. A poetics is initiated with language as a passport, a magical entry to "an alternate universe." History, travel, and autobiography are all the occasion of these crossing points, these corners turned to find that yellow translates from the Sahara to the old neighborhood. Dove's poetics has a palette of colors and a geometry that "proves" with a liberating rigor and yeastiness that "the [yellow] house expands." In mixing metaphors from the poems "Geometry" and "Ö" here, my intention is to emphasize that they are both important figural sources for Dove's art. Youthfully ardent and euphoric, these poems are signatures of an aspiring poet yet also realized achievements. For the book is also an opening, as if striking a key, giving a motif, in the musical form and the mythic dimensions of her imagination that are set in train here as if to give notice of compositional intention. That the collection is organized in five suites with a poem titled "A Suite for Augustus" at its core is a significant formal marker of connection with variation as the key to the composing of a volume.

To invoke a musical vocabulary is not to forget another aspect of the collection, the cool, analytical mind that is in evidence here. Techniques such as dramatized speakers, interior monologue, and disjunctive storytelling in short sequences give insight into the signifying aspects of culture as it saturates the adolescent, the lover, and the traveler, past or present. The effect is to reveal the ideologies of gender, race, and power that inhabit consciousness. By these strategies, the personal is not abstracted but located within the cultural.

Dove's agenda for creating her own poetic identity is, at times, explicit. An important part of this volume is her research into African American history. This empathy with black American origins is a significant "identity marker,"[15] not merely a dutiful acknowledgment. The imaginative exploration of history yields considerable artistic dividends: through the process of historical recovery, she develops an antiphonal mode of expressing contrasting voices. Her poetry, in linking different perspectives, animates and reassesses them.

CHAPTER 3

Museum

Bringing Dark Wood to Life

If *The Yellow House on the Corner* ends on an upbeat note, Dove's next volume, *Museum,* is an altogether flintier artifact, the product of a dig into cultural origins that is, at times, discomforting.[1] *Museum* is less buoyant than *The Yellow House on the Corner,* more ruthless in its inspections. It would be an exaggeration to say that in the first part of *Museum* the past is a rubbish dump submitted to the American imperial gaze, but it is certainly passed under a candid review, and not without mordant humor. There are, of course, continuities with the first volume, most notably in the delight in fable and legend. If the past is a collection of artifacts, it is also the stories about them that succeeding generations reshape. Dove is very conscious of the paradox of the historicist imagination that seeks to recover the otherness of the past yet also looks for, or unexpectedly finds, its own reflection.

The poems in part 1, "The Hill Has Something to Say," are mainly about Europe, at one level tourist reflections upon classical Greece and medieval Italy, meditations on the two-way exchange between past and present, and explorations of the gaps in ideology and belief that the long fall through time has created. The epigraph from a modern American tombstone of the aptly named (for an exemplary narrator) Ike Tell in Weimar, Texas, is an ironic reminder of the ideological discrepancies between the modern and medieval mind. Living in a world unframed by God, or indeed, gods, foreshortens the modern imaginative take on the primary worlds of earlier times.

Skeletal Blossom from the Past

The first poem of part 1, "The Fish in the Stone," acts at one level as a reminder of distance and of the intricacies of evolution that have brought the past into the orbit of our inspection. As a Darwinian meditation upon process, the poem turns on the ironies of the fossil record as evidence of life. The petrification that guarantees or provides proof of the lived existence is the opposite of the vitality of that existence. Such paradoxes are evident in the beautifully judged opening, bare, almost laconic in expression:

> The fish in the stone
> would like to fall
> back into the sea.

The lines suggest not only the idea that the fossilized fish might like to avoid exemplary status as specimen but also the twist of fate that might have led to the living fish being thrown back by an angler. The weariness of the fish stems from its desire to slip back into the anonymity of the sea to escape the burden of analysis. Such ambiguities of meaning, poised between mutability and permanence, structure the poem: "the moment comes" for the fish "to cast his / skeletal blossom," as if the fossil image is both a shedding of life and the making of a sculptural art form. Similarly, the fish

> knows to fail is
> to do the living
> a favor.

These lines have a precise lineation and exactitude of thought reminiscent of the famous poem "The Fish" by the modernist Marianne Moore.[2] Dove's fossil-fish acquires the wisdom of ages, knows of the evolutionary struggle in which his death leaves more chance for the other fish to survive, but also knows that as a relic he does the scientist of the future "a favor." Like the "voluptuous braille" of the fern, another primitive form, the fossil image is a transmuted language that can be decoded. Such paradoxes are the symbolic expression of the exchanges of nature and culture that structure the poem.

The Poem as Museum

The ambiguities of "The Fish in the Stone," the slippages from flux to fixity, from nature to culture, are also structurally significant as a focus for the first part of the volume, an exploration of paradoxes inherent in the concept of a museum. If a museum is a storehouse of knowledge, the mausoleum of the past, its original meaning is the seat of the Muses, a creative source. Similarly, a poem (a "thing made" in its original meaning) is the completed artifact, the "dead" fossil relic of the process of creativity. Dove's poem might be read as a poetics in registering the process of patience, drift, and "engineering" by which the fossil poem is "cast." The figural suggestiveness of the poem is its potential to become that paradoxical feat, a "skeletal blossom." Ambiguity of language enables the poem to live in its "dead" state, although the "analysis" it encounters from the reader might be "small." In larger terms, the implicit analogies between the processes of nature and the cultural work of the poet whose labor is fossilized in the poem itself are energies that work against the inertia of time. The poem creates a dynamic between present and past. As such, it acts as a portal to the explorations of subsequent poems that are about reading the past and coming into active imaginative relationship with it.

The Feminine Breath of History

The four poems that follow have Greek subject matter: the sensory experiences of tourism and the modern encounter with classical ruins in "The Ants of Argos," the cool interior of a stone jar in "Pithos." "Nestor's Bathtub" is a comic exposé of the manipulations of legend that tourism generates and that then become self-sustaining (it was Nestor's wife, not Nestor, who used the bathtub). "The Hill Has Something to Say" is a witty variant on the romantic notion of a correspondent breeze in nature and humanity. The act of climbing the hill initiates the process of taking in the past. Inspiration is a taking in of breath, of inhaling sound that is itself "amphoric," already shaped by culture. The word "amphoric" means the sound produced by blowing or speaking into an amphora, the two-handled vessel for wine or oil, and thus expresses both the living breath and the finished artifact. The poem echoes with human and atmospheric exchanges: the wind "groans," its breath "pacing / our lungs." The hill is nature, yet the shape of the land is human, referred to as if a human figure. Yet it is also a rubbish dump, a compacted jumble, in the same way as language is a mix of kinds of stories, mythology, folk tale, and nursery rhyme. The title of the poem "The Hill Has Something to Say" runs into the first line, "but isn't talking," and is the implied preceding line for all the subsequent stanzas. The relics exposed by "Scavenger Time" need energetic retrieval.

"The Hill Has Something to Say" is succeeded by a group of narrative vignettes, or "pruned" legends, to pick up a metaphor from the poem "The Copper Beech," that are versions of the past speaking to us. The poems dramatize the minds of legendary figures, mostly feminine, and experiment with stanza forms that both compress the narrative and, by artful enjambment, lead the reader through a showing forth of the mind of the protagonist. As a historicist imagining of the protocols of the past, a poem such as "Tou Wan Speaks to Her Husband, Liu Sheng" is intimate and tender. It enacts the ritual funeral observances followed by the wife of this princely ruler who died in 113 B.C.E. Tou Wan speaks reverently yet frankly to her husband about her arrangements for his house of death. She takes him on a guided tour of the burial chamber, tactfully noting that though the size is limited, it will last "forever" (in the note to the poem, Dove points out that the tomb was unearthed in 1968). The symbolism of the objects placed in the tomb, such as the "chariot" for the journey, is matched by practicality: the incense burner is to allay "the stench of your / own diminishing." The arrangements are fitted to the magnificence of a great man, but the wife knows how "bored" and fretful he will be at this containment, this diminishment of scale in a dark place. And so, again with exquisite tact, Tou Wan speaks tranquilly of the time "when you are long light and clouds / over the earth, just as the legends prophesy."

Tou Wan's role, as the submissive imperial wife, contrasts with the more rugged individualism of the two saints in "Catherine of Alexandria" and "Catherine of Siena." These poems have a skeptical yet sympathetic feminist voice conscious of the sensual deprivations and hardships that shape the capacity for sainthood. Thus in "Catherine of Alexandria," the modern speaker, reflecting on the narrowness of the saint's life as a young girl, deduces that this must have been a case of sexuality transmuted into the passion of Christ. In contrast, another Saint

Catherine, in "Catherine of Siena," has a masculine resolve (in terms of the expectations of medieval society) to travel, to put herself in danger in her search for God.

Dove's experiments with dramatic monologues that characterize speakers of earlier historical periods are indicative of her desire to enter sympathetically into the cultural codes of the past while also injecting a measure of realism into the expression. This is particularly effective in "Tou Wan Speaks to Her Husband, Liu Sheng," which blends an understanding of the ways in which any wife would be intimate with the characteristics of her husband with a fine sense of the larger belief system in which that individual experience is grounded. The majority of the speakers or protagonists of these poems are women in circumscribed conditions. In the case of the saints, it could be said that the rebellion, in taking a religious form, finds a traditional outlet for eccentricity. The interest of the poet is in how these legendary figures were human, and how she, as a modern poet, can find a succinct narrative form that will highlight both the myth and the quiddity of their existence as it can be imagined.

The Eye of the Outsider

As an American studying in Germany and as a black American, standing out from the norm in appearance, Dove was drawn to speculate on exceptionality, the ways in which an individual is differentiated from the mass and the extent to which such qualities can be transplanted into another culture. In an interview, she commented on the meanings of "In the Bulrush," the subtitle of the second part of *Museum:* "It has obvious religious connotations of Moses, but also the idea about becoming a chosen one from the weeds, an unlikely place to be lifted out of and to make an impact."[3]

The first three poems extend that idea to translation from one sphere or language to another and consider the potential in seeing things askew, learning aslant, or impacting on a different culture. "Shakespeare Say," as Dove says in her note to the poem, is about the black American blues singer, Champion Jack Dupree, living and touring in Europe. This larger-than-life personality has a Falstaffian gusto considerably dampened by the German weather, which gives an extra lugubrious edge to his blues. The poem has an alternating pattern of blues and comic accounts of his almost royal progress. Champion Jack adjusts his material to the circumstances, so that his current numbers have a Shakespearian endorsement. The poem draws to a close in the mode of a blues set that comes together:

> Going down slow
> crooning *Shakespeare say*
> *man must be*
> *careful what he kiss*
> *when he drunk,*
> going down
> for the third set

Champion Jack seems here not only the myth but also the natural man for whom the blues are intrinsic expression, even this far from Louisiana. The poem is deceptively simple: one of the experiments with the "shorter line . . . poems with slim silhouettes"[4] that Dove instigated while writing *Museum* yet evocative in the juxtaposition of flamboyant image and lachrymose song, "with a red eye / for women" "crowing . . . *poor me / poor me.*" Just as the blues singer is both magnificently out of place and an extraordinary translation of idiom, so the poem plays off the idiom of the blues. Dove's comic empathy with her subject had its roots in her own sense of displacement while living in Germany in the 1970s.

A similar contrast of scale and kinds of cultural vision is evident in considering the poems "At the German Writers Conference in Munich" and "Banneker."

The former, in terse note form, represents a black writer's eye scanning a medieval tapestry with a modern union banner tacked across it, "taut and white / as skin (not mine)." The Aryan ethos, taken for granted but obtrusive to a black observer, is evident in the rather sickly idiom of the tapestry, the "ash-blonde princess," white horse and white doves. The poet speculates on the Latin inscription of the medieval tapestry and the unlikelihood that it would record the Jewish dyers and the wives who made it. The stretched "skin" of the banner evokes the racist ideologies underlying the selective characteristics of the tapestry, which to a nonwhite "pokes out." The verb is deliberately crude to counter the anodyne prettiness of the picture.

The assumption in "At the German Writers Conference in Munich," that writers will conform to the dominant ideology, contrasts with the mold-breaking freedom of "Banneker," the first black man to predict a solar eclipse:

> What did he do except lie
> under a pear tree, wrapped in
> a great cloak, and meditate
> on the heavenly bodies?

This is an American idiom of self-sufficiency and vision. Banneker was also appointed (as Dove informs us in the notes to the poem) to the commission planning the city that became Washington, D.C. His passionate energy, whether penning an "enflamed letter" to Jefferson, figuratively shooting at the stars, or envisaging a city "spreading / in a spiral of lights," is celebrated, as is his idiosyncracy. Banneker is one of those "capacious" figures who contribute to the space and range of the self-creating mythology of Americanness. He comes out of nowhere, like the unknown escaping black slave in "Three Days of Forest, a River, Free," with a toughness of spirit that embraces opportunity.

A number of poems in *Museum* posit an American largeness of spirit that, in exceptional cases, can overcome segregation, deprivation, or displacement. But Dove is also aware of the negative aspects of exceptionality in any form, the fate of people who are culturally defined as hardly human but also as exotic oddities, like museum exhibits. Christian Schad's 1929 portrait, "Agosta the Winged Man and Rasha the Black Dove," is of two such individuals. Dove's poem of the same title is a response to the painting.

Ekphrasis and Exhibition

Agosta and Rasha were sideshow entertainers in Berlin in the 1920s. Rasha, from Madagascar, performed an act with a boa constrictor, and Agosta's bone deformity was in itself sufficient spectacle. Rasha's blackness and Agosta's physical frame marked them out as freaks. They were, as an act, already on show for the populace, cruelly distinguished from normality. A painting, however, necessarily precipitates the individual into a different kind of visibility, the frame of high art. Dove's poem imagines Schad working out how to place them for the portrait.

Paradoxically, the visual shape of her poem, the vertical short line format with linear and syntactical variation, undermines the fixity of visual staging, whether that of popular entertainment or of painting. The line placing, the turn of one line into the next, the stretching and contracting of the stanza length, are integral to the strategy of tracing the process of thinking that precedes the "frozen" image of the portrait. The details in the poem of Schad's studio, the glimpses of the everyday existence of his two models, and his memories of the stories of their past lives combine to hold off the moment of fixity, the decision to settle on a particular pose. The shifts of perspective and location in the poem have a visual equivalence in the enjambment shrinking and extending, a cultural elasticity that holds off exhibition. The painter, however, had to deal head on with the issue of whether there was a moral difference in exhibiting them in an art gallery rather than a fairground. Could there be an objective but not an objectifying representation? The poem defers the answer, keeps open a narrative, and thus intrinsically more human and socialized dimension, to their lives, but the painting is a more exigent visualization, characteristic of the realism of the Neue Sachlichkeit[5] movement of the 1920s.

The figures in Schad's portraits are often exposed in tense proximity with a realism that compounds the ambiguities of the juxtapositions. This is particularly the case with the portrait of Agosta and Rasha. The dimensions of the painting, 120 by 80 centimeters, are modest as befitted the sober utility of the new realism, as if to give them dignity without inflation, seriousness without indignity. They are placed in a studio. Agosta is seated in three-quarter pose on a chair of classicized art nouveau design, his chest exposed with classical drapery on the lower part of his body. His discarded black coat hangs over one arm of the chair. Rasha, in the foreground in a bust-length full-face pose, wears a dress of a folk motif pattern.

For a modern spectator, their isolation from a social context cannot help but call their identity into question in a bleakly resonant way. The fate of the two performers in Germany in the thirties is likely to have been dire, and to the retrospective eye the somber gaze of Agosta and Rasha in the portrait is premonitory of their fate, or the fate of those like them in the Nazi era. However, hindsight also makes it possible to read the portrait as a caricature of racist arrogance or, indeed, of ethnic cleansing in the hauteur of Agosta and the subservient lower position of Rasha. Agosta's bone disease is thereby, in its jutting extrusions and concavities, a symbol of self-destructing *imperium*. Equally plausibly, one might read the emaciated white man's displacement by the healthy black woman in the foreground as a symptom of cultural decay and renewal. It is difficult not to read the painting in terms of racialized and gendered power, yet the irony is that Schad wanted to remove the subjects from abnormality, from marginality, to represent them with objectivity.

Dove's own concern in coming across the painting at a gallery in Berlin in 1982[6] and finding that the woman not only looked like her but also had the same name, and understanding that being black in 1929 Berlin was a deformity, is *not* expressed in her poem. In this respect, she sought a parallel objectivity to the painting in her representation, editing out her own feelings. It is significant, however, that "merciless" is the last word in the poem: it is attributed to the gaze of the two sitters, but the process of the poem has been, in part, to sift, to discriminate between different kinds of spectatorship. It investigates how ways of looking are ways of stereotyping, of objectifying the subject. The poem is about such reification, but it also seeks to work another way in what Dove called her "starburst fashion,"[7] the snippets of detail about the lives of Rasha and Agosta recalled in Schad's musing process.

The poem begins, "Schad paced the length of his studio" and then shifts perspective from inside to outside, to the Hardenbergstrasse, where Agosta and Rasha pose in their sideshow. As the painter thinks of their performance, the lines uncoil like the act with the boa constrictor:

> How
> the spectators gawked, exhaling
> beer and sour herring sighs. . . .
> The canvas,
>
> not his eye, was merciless.

The spectators are themselves momentarily like clumsy peasants in a Brueghel painting, "exhaling / beer and sour herring."

The distinction made in the last sentence of the quotation is an aesthetic, an intellectual distinction, but the difficulty of making it in the present case is signaled by the isolating of "The canvas" and the gap before "not his eye." The hiatus of the stanza break registers the unease, the need to make the distinction. The poet, personally assailed by the pictorial image, needs to reassure herself that the act of transference of the image is not complicit with the gawking of the crowd. She would like to remove both the painter and the poet from the charge. But the charge always hangs in the air, and even if the artist is not "merciless," the canvas is. At this point, halfway through the poem, the statement functions ambiguously. Is it a moral get-out clause (it is not the human creator but the end product that is "merciless") or, more compromisingly, is the rapacity merely transferred from eye to canvas? And the canvas, like the sideshow, generates spectators who will appropriate and invest the image in their own ways.

As the poem proceeds, the issue of investment is developed. With what shall these figures be invested? The poet, in tracking the painter's thought processes as he recalls that other "arena" in which Agosta has been displayed as an exhibit to medical students, "his torso exposed / its crests and fins" like "a colony of birds." The pathos of Agosta's predicament, his spirit trapped in disfigurement, is one response narrative can allow, as it can also connect Rasha with warmth, giving them both human particularity. The careful spacing of the lines of the poem defers indignation and anger on their behalf and ultimately decides against it. Hot lust, beery breath, compassion—these they have always been subjected to in their exhibited lives. The final lines seem to accept the validity of the painter's classical composition, "without passion." If art is going to join in the spectating game, it should clear itself of conferring pity or sentiment, those self-exonerating spectatorial emotions. Classical detachment is appropriate, too, for figures accustomed to being much looked at. The outcome is that Agosta and Rasha, at the end of the poem, acquire an uncompromising monumentality:

> Not
> the canvas
> but their gaze,
> so calm,
> was merciless.

The "gaze" is now symbolically transferred from the painter's art, the "canvas," to the subjects themselves, who hold and distance the spectator.

Nevertheless, it is of course the painter's art, the canvas, that achieves this reversal of roles. The transferences of responsibility that structure the poem are not to be altogether believed. The portrait is of an emotive subject, and the poem is about the decisions that the painter would have made before he could say to himself, "Agosta in / classical drapery, then." Dove's poem is about process and product, and in imagining the stages of Schad's thoughts, she can displace her own, more personal responses to the painting: "Without passion" is a decision shared by painter and poet. The poem about the painting will be similarly dispassionate.

Ut pictura poesis[8] then? Not quite in this case, or not without distinctions to be made. The poem is as much about the differences between the two arts as about their analogies. But in that the poem is always working with the relationships between the verbal and visual, the term *ekphrasis*[9] is appropriate. Further, although it is a poem with narrative elements, the visual shape acts as a boundary to the desire to soften, to fill in the edges of the lives that the portrait eliminates. The narrative mode is checked by the exactitude of the lineation and by the stanzas, which, although irregular, with lines stepping out, nevertheless collect the anecdotal into the compositional demands of the form. The poem, then, can admit but limit the anecdote that permits another kind of visual image, such as Rasha with "fresh eggs . . . flecked and warm as breath." The poem does not have to freeze into one frame.

Nevertheless, as it hones down to the close, the poem honors the more exigent discipline of portrait painting, matching its clarity and austerity. Schad's thinking process has been registered, but, significantly, Dove's has not. Neither her personal feelings about Schad's image nor her thinking process about how to structure her own work are in the poem. As she has intuited about Schad's portrait, this was not an occasion for emotional intrusion. In the final image, then, hard won, *ut pictura poesis*.

Dove, in finding herself in the portrait of Rasha, the black dove, has nevertheless acknowledged Rasha's "Otherness" in the "other room" of the painting as it symbolizes her separate life, not to be appropriated personally or polemically and only, "without passion," artistically. Furthermore, commenting on the poem, Dove said that she wanted to begin with Schad thinking of Agosta and Rasha, "how aware they are of their Otherness."[10]

In omitting the autobiographical quest, the identity crisis, Dove has kept the temperature low. The "chill" authority of the resolute finish seems especially earned as the poetic voice converges with or overlays the painting in the final lines. The statement "not the canvas" either concurs with the step back to acknowledge the agency of the subjects or the poem displaces the canvas as a representation.

Dove's ekphrastic procedures, however, are not quite as clear cut as the resolution of statement seems to suggest. Her poem is ironic about its own procedures. The closing eight lines seem to resolve contradiction as they express the placing of the models, opening thus:

> Agosta in
> classical drapery, then,
> And Rasha at his feet.
> Without passion. Not

But the hanging "Not" is not presiding over an act of settlement in the following lines. The last four lines are visually and verbally at odds with one another:

> the canvas
>
> > > but their gaze,
> > > so calm,
> >
> > was merciless.

The left justification on the page of "canvas" and "merciless," so that the eye is as likely to look down as across, is a reminder that earlier in the poem it was the canvas that was merciless. Just as the poem seems to have settled everything by displacements that distance responsibility, the doubt is allowed back in. The visual layout keeps the qualms about who is merciless before us.

Dove's poem is ekphrastic in the broad sense, as James A. W. Heffernan describes it, in being the "verbal representation of visual representation." Heffernan goes on to say that ekphrasis "evokes the power of the silent image even as it subjects that power to the rival authority of language."[11] Dove's version is less antagonistic than he postulates. She is aware that the cultural sensitivity of the subjects of Schad's painting poses a sharp question about why they should be brought into the museum of art, or into "the museum of words," to pick up Heffernan's title phrase. Put simply, she wants them represented as human beings, not oddities, yet the poem is also faithful to history: the very *juxtaposition* of Agosta and Rasha is a reminder that in 1929 in Berlin they were bracketed as oddities. Dove's poem is, therefore, not so much a struggle for language to rival the authority of the painting, rather, the language seeks an equivalent self-authorization. The struggle, in the poem as in the painting, is to justify the representation. Thus, although Dove's narrative elements underline the differences in method between poetry and painting, her poem is ideologically coincident with

Schad's painting. Both painter and poet have resolved ideological problems in their aesthetics of representation. Equally
important, the ekphrastic act of the poem activates the links
between the two art forms. In Heffernan's words,

> We do well to remember the root meaning of ekphrasis:
> "speaking out" or "telling in full." To recall this root mean-
> ing is to recognize that besides representational friction and
> the turning of fixed forms into narrative, ekphrasis entails
> prosopopoeia, or the rhetorical technique of envoicing a
> silent object. Ekphrasis speaks not only *about* works of art
> but also *to* and *for* them.[12]

In Dove's poem, in accordance with her declared principles in
Museum, she speaks not only *for* the painting but also for its
human subjects, who "can't speak to us anymore."[13] But this is
no easy take over bid. What is notable, when she has annexed
this painting into her museum of words, is the power that she
leases back to it. At the end of her poem, the poet attributes to
the painting the very power that words do not have. She
reminds us that it is a silent static object. The painting has not
tried to round out the lives of Agosta and Rasha and, in not
speaking for them but isolating them, it has been truer to the
cultural conditions of their existence. The reversal of roles, in
that they seem to gaze at the spectator as mercilessly as they
have been "gawked" at, is a visual effect, the impact of which
the poet can hardly match. It is as much in these secessions as in
the annexations that Dove's poem retains its full ekphrastic
potential.

The section of the volume *Museum* titled "In the Bulrush,"
which includes "Agosta the Winged Man and Rasha the Black

Dove," takes the "rainbow" of its Bob Marley epigraph with seriousness and grace: the critique of color as the basis of cultural separatism is matched by an exploration of the power of art to reproduce or to question such divisions. The reifying, potentially deadening objectifications of art, its museum mode, is equally under scrutiny. Art is not necessarily miraculous salvation or rainbow promise, and to translate from one culture to another is to be painfully aware of the stultifying ways in which individuals become "other" and thus no longer individual. A number of the poems in this section seem to be a breaking of the "shell"[14] of stereotyping. They are aware of the capacity of art to seem complicit with a dominant ideology, and, knowing themselves to be capable of treachery, they warily express the relational tensions between cultures in the tensions between visual and verbal representation. Other poems, such as "Shakespeare Say," by their very rhythm translate freely across cultures and create, in the juxtaposed incongruities, a rich remixing.

Writing the Father

The vantage point of the third part of *Museum,* "My Father's Telescope," is, as the epigraph from a Bessie Smith blues suggests, the "hill" from which a different perspective of one's roots can be taken. The sequence of poems that follows are rooted in Dove's Akron, Ohio, childhood: "All my beginning memories come out of my experiences in Akron. . . . It's not true to write about some place that doesn't have that emotional resonance for you. . . . Akron is my own."[15] The poems have a specificity of sensory detail, an anecdotal pleasure that evoke belonging, place in the sense of a secure identity, a *familiar* location. Within so much that is known, the poet recognizes the unknown elements of her father in the title of the section and the lead poem, "My Father's Telescope": "My father is someone that I've had a hard time understanding. Sometimes he seemed like another planet, very far away. And to draw him closer was also part of the sense of that title."[16] The idea of the telescope therefore combines studying him as a feature of her childhood topography, bringing a distant object close, but also trying to understand his viewpoint, as if looking out from his, at times, frustrated perspective. The title also connects with the final part of the volume, which expands from the personal to the global. Dove was writing the poems during the period in which satellite images of Saturn and Jupiter were beamed back to Earth, so the whole section is informed by the sense that near and far are contiguous, capable of being connected.

The first poem, "Grape Sherbet," is threaded by a Proustian joke, a memory of a childhood occasion in which the poet's father made grape sherbet; the taste to the children was like "lavender" or "salt on a melon," but to the adult trying to remember, the taste "doesn't exist." It is not the taste that brings back the memory. Instead, this is a deliberate effort to exhibit her father's character. The word "Memorial" in the first line is appropriate to the fact that the day was a special one, a visit to the family graves. The poem itself is a kind a formal memorializing in art, an incongruous fixing of that which, like the sherbet, is evanescent, with a comic touch in suggesting the paternal ego. There are no confessional hatreds here, just a touch of good-humored rivalry as if to say, Daddy, producer of the "masterpiece" of sherbet, this poem is *my* emperor of ice cream.[17] What lasts, though, is the idea of family continuity, the belief that it matters:

> Now I see why
> you bothered,
> father.

Existence is perpetuated in caring memory and memory is formally carried in art. The care with which the sherbet was constructed in all its fragility is the same kind of caring that ensures important things are not forgotten. The poem plays lightly on its Stevensian themes of sensory delight, transience, and death, as if Wallace Stevens's idealist austerity had been touched with family exuberance. For Dove, as for Stevens, the poem is the paradoxical memorial of that which melts away yet is also the renewal of its occasion.

An autobiographical series of poems by a female poet in search of a father stimulates comparison with Sylvia Plath's more agonized but equally crafted endeavor to "put together" her father. Plath's poem "The Colossus" evokes a ruin, yet a building site in which the poet, "scaling little ladders," reconstructs her father and inserts herself into the literary canon. Plath's linking of the personal and the political was more savage, of course, in "Daddy,"[18] her dramatization of the paternal as hateful tyrant, figured in terms of the Nazi jack-boot, violence generating violence. In her more imagistic poem "Ariel," the personal was melted down into the mythical. Dove's enterprise is closer to Plath's emotional range and scale in her mythic series *Mother Love* (1995), yet the crafting of the father poems in *Museum* owes much to the achievement of Plath's generation. The artificial barrier between formalism and a confessional or autobiographical mode had been dismantled, as Dove has commented:

> These battles have already been fought. And these are not
> easy battles—between confessionalism and beat poetry and

formalism, or whether poetry adheres to gender or not, or whether it adheres to whatever black aesthetics. These discussions have been on the table. We haven't had to clear the path first before writing.[19]

The poems about Dove's father, for all their intertextual resonance and awareness of the literary traditions of autobiography and memory, also depict a father with a definite character: his passion for rose growing is referred to again in the 1993 poem "In the Old Neighborhood," which prefaces *Selected Poems,* in which he is described as a man who "each summer . . . brandishes color / over the neighborhood." In "Roses," the savagery of his obsession in combating predators and in hungrily shaping the destiny of his prize cultivars is comically expressed in his pruning shears as a "mammoth claw resting between meals." Both "Roses" and "Grape Sherbet" portray a man of intense, even rigid, standards of attainment, as if the frustrations of his professional life are partially vented in the intensity of these domestic activities.

Dove's father trained as an industrial chemist, the first black chemist to qualify in the Goodyear Tire Company in Akron, but the company barred him for a considerable time from working in that professional capacity. Instead, he had to work as an elevator man. These biographical details are not mentioned in the poems; they express a child's perspective in a domestic context. "Roses," in particular, represents Dove as a child, bewildered by the "flat dark fury" of the father's face, as she is forced to participate in the slaughter of the beetles infesting his beloved roses. The color scheme of the poem delivers a Blakean antithesis, a clash between the "pinkish eyelids of the roses" and the "dark fury" of their preserver. Blakean, too, is the fact that the disease-carrying beetles come from Japan (the episode is dated 1961), as if another vengeful twist to the war and blight between the two countries. The savagery with which the father destroys the beetles in order to produce a perfect "inculpable" rose is a metaphor for global combat yet also a personal displacement of frustrated energy that terrifies the uncomprehending child. The group of poems about her father captures how the harshness in his character is part of a scientific determination to explore and know. Paternal protector or ruthless educator, a father is a metamorphic being.

The poem "My Father's Telescope" is a sympathetic rendering of her father's attempts to contain his talents within the domestic frame by developing his carpentry skills. But after "years of cupboards" and dutiful "elves . . . in snow" for the kids, his attempt to make a three-legged chair fails. There is a comic sexual subtext to the poem in the playful image of the father's attempts to accommodate his masculinity to the small compass that "shrinks" his desires. His masculine quest for a horizon beyond the domestic is sublimated into the purchase of a telescope ostensibly for his son's Christmas present. The sense of cosmic escape and enviable enlargement that the telescope provides for the son is evident in the next poem, "Song, Summer," in which the brother swoops "sexless" over the house, liberated from culture and nature by the range of the telescope. It is a paradoxically gendered escape from gender, as only the males are granted this release, this flight from the quotidian. The foregoing poems have shown something of the irritated spirit self-disciplined, shy, yet yearning for greater tests, the paradoxes of paternal and sexual energies that have to be contained within this other planet of masculinity. This is a reminder that these poems are a daughter's scrutiny not only of a father but also of a man, and of a constructive and visually exploratory intelligence (in father and son) not so unlike her own.

Indeed, the poem "Anti-Father" dares to take issue with the oracle on points of astronomy, asserting the right of the daughter to be on equal intellectual terms as well as to be "woman to man." The poem begins with the word "Contrary," but it is not aggressive. The thirteen two-line stanzas of only two, three, or four words in each line with a final one-word line are a meticulously phrased meditation on the spaces and intimacies that the planetary systems suggest about the father-daughter relationship. The poem conceives of two notions of time, the first being the human scale of natural decay, the dilapidation of the house as Wordsworthian emblem of culture returning to nature. The shriveling is also emblematic of the father's loss of scale and authority as the child becomes adult. The other notion of time, the larger-scale understanding that can only be conceptual rather than observed, is the knowledge that

> the stars
> are not far
>
> apart. Rather
> they draw
>
> closer together
> with years.

The finely placed separations and proximities of the words are images of the unseen, unspoken thought processes that have to be deduced in exploring the mysteries of another person. The ambiguities of enjambments such as "not far / apart" that venture across the blank into the next verse are as productive as any of the simplicities of Robert Frost: "not far" suggests near, but the phrase falls into the space of "apart," meaning separated but also, paradoxically, fleetingly, it suggests "a part of." The formal play of meanings, the biological conception opposed to the unexpected or inconceivable feeling of intimacy with him in visualizing "outer space," is finely handled in the closing lines of the poem:

> Just between
>
> me and you,
> woman to man,
>
> outer space is
> inconceivably
>
> intimate.

What is particularly finely judged is that there is no collapse down into sentimental alignment: the measured transmission is "me" to "you," "woman to man." It is scrupulously a one-way insight mediated by the idea that a vast distance might be perceived as intimate. The paradox that her father has conceived her, but that it is inconceivable to be directly physically intimate with this reserved man who seems to exist in a world of his own, remains. The word "between" stands out at the end of the line and the stanza as a check on the casual intimacy that seems to be introduced by "Just between." The art of the poem lies in the upholding of formal distance. Even phrases such as "me and you" and "woman to man" are given "outer space" on the page, as if with ceremonious enhancement. They stand symbolically, rather than cosily, together. The final paradoxical conceit in which the analogy between the inconceivability of "outer space" becoming "intimate" and her father's universe coming imaginatively in the lens retains the mystery of both, yet with the proximal understanding that time is not linear but all around us. This is a more awesome sense of family relationship, not as succession but as being like time, "un-lost," ubiquitous, discounting conventional notions of far and near.

The poems in the third part of the volume, "My Father's Telescope," are held within the central imagery of the distanced vision of that title. The telescope can bring selected outward detail of distant objects into view, but it does not actually bring them any closer; they are not in touching distance. The image therefore respects the idea of distance and does not try to assume or force intimacy. There is a compelling emotional honesty in the rectitude of this aspect of the image. Furthermore, as the blues epigraph to the third part reminds us, maturity and the understanding it brings of the "lonesome" nature of adult life enables us to look back to childhood and understand that our parents had aspirations and frustrations outside those concerned with our own upbringing. In this respect, distance confers empathy. The continuum between the vast and the familiar is comforting. In the fourth and last part of the volume, this continuum is addressed in historical terms.

History

History, as Dove gave notice in *The Yellow House on the Corner*, is one of her most significant interests. In *Thomas and Beulah*, her family history becomes an exemplary American history, her African American Akron succeeding Robert Lowell's Brahmin Boston as literary locale and lens for the nation to learn about itself. In the fourth and last part of *Museum*, "Primer for the Nuclear Age," Dove looks also to the larger, more global patterns of history, the patterns of imperialism, the perpetrators and victims of slavery, the cycles of injustice and enterprise. The past has lessons for us, yet the stretch of the title is ironic, as the past can hardly be expected to furnish forth a basic survival kit for the present. Indeed, the poems of this section do not have an axe to grind in relation to the politics of the past. The perspective ranges from a historical overview to being inside the head of a dictator, but these are cool and witty poems, not angry polemics. In an interview with Therese Steffen, Dove emphasized her artistic position: "My writing is not propagandistic. . . . This is not the concern of the artist. It would falsify the writing itself to figure out the implications beforehand; not only would it narrow artistic expression, but the very essence of art would be compromised. . . . I'm not an insistent or indignant sort of writer."[20]

The subject of "The Sailor in Africa," the opening poem of "Primer for the Nuclear Age," is imperialism and the vicissitudes of the slave trade. The subtitle informs us that the poem is based on "*a Viennese card game, circa 1910*," and it is the witty tension between the historical narrative and the strict schema of the card game that generates the ironies of this account of colonial enterprise. The poem is ludic in structure and in tone. The narrator's explanation of the rules of the game imposes a detached vision of the historical scenario: "The goal is Africa." The captains of the four ships are the active counters in the game or, to put it another way, represent the nations competing for slaves. They are themselves categorized as "white" (the British and French captains) and "Moors" (the Italian and Spanish captains). The pilots of the vessels "complement their superiors" in color. The crews, of course, are "motley." Both card games and individual enterprise are subject to chance, the throw of the dice.

Given the emotive and politically flagrant nature of the subject matter, it is a considerable feat to maintain a consistently comic perspective, in part by the fiction of adherence to the rules, moves, and chance of the game:

> Say the Italian Moor
> sails in sunshine
> to Morocco and is rewarded
> five black chips.

The rewards are slaves, but there is also admiration for the swashbuckling enterprise of the protagonists, the readiness of such men to face the reversals as well as to seek the prizes of fortune. For example, Pedro, the Spanish captain, finds himself at one stage sold as a slave to the French captain. Escaping, however, and in his next enterprise heading for the "prodigious" women of Brazil, Pedro is last heard of in a massive storm at sea, the ship splintering on the rocks "just as" the "black hand" of the Italian captain, abandoned in the Madagascan forest by his crew, lifts a bright green egg from a nest. History will get it all wrong of course: the crew that has betrayed the Italian captain will report his "untimely demise."

The national characteristics are deftly registered in vignettes of the fastidious hauteur of the French, the amorous Spaniard, the lustful Italian, and the English captain, red-eyed from staring at the sun. The poem ends with the English captain, wind stalled in the Atlantic, reduced to "playing cards" to pass the time. Many felicities in the poem arise from the ludic combinations and contrasts of regulation and chance, commerce and

nature, individuality and typicality, history and fate. The lightness of touch does not preclude moments suggestive of epic
grandeur, as when Pedro glimpses

> through the storm's
> pearly membrane
> God's dark face swooping
> down to kiss

This is temperament, history and fate rolled into one, a reminder
that such enterprises were at the physical and spiritual edge of
existence, open to delirious sensations unknown to decorous
Viennese card players.

"The Sailor in Africa" is a narrative poem of considerable
originality. The artfulness of the form contains the narrative
swell of the sea yarn within the discipline of the run of cards:
this in itself is subtly metafictional. The card game and the
adventure story have each their conventions within which risks
are dealt and played out. Historical narrative has also conventions that the wild card of individuality sometimes eludes, like
the "black hand" in the Madagascan forest that does not conform to cultural expectations. The narrator, this laconic explica-
tor of the games of narrative, history, and cards, displays in each
of these elements the characteristics of the others, teasing the
reader into decoding the spatial and linear patterns created. To
view colonial history with the artistic detachment of this poem
is like observing through a telescope, and the image of the telescope is appropriate, too, for the selection of detail brought into
sharp focus. Similarly, for the reader to follow the artful moves
of the narrative is like participating in a game of cards, trying to
keep up with several strands of play. The card game is itself a
microcosm, a self-declared model of imperialist competition.

Dove conflates the discourses of imperialist adventure and of didactic explication to create an ironic mode in which the clichés of both discourses are relished and made salient by juxtaposition. The effect is revitalization rather than satiric dismissal. The narrator reenters those ways of thinking and feeling, those disjunctions between European drawing room and African jungle that so tormented Joseph Conrad in *Heart of Darkness,* his novella of 1902. By 1910, the darkness could easily be packaged for the drawing room. Dove seems to find this illuminating rather than reprehensible and, with a Bakhtinian[21] ear for the intrinsically dialogic nature of narrative, imports the languages of these different speech communities parodically, with the slight intensifications that stylize them. Thus the intellectual schematizing discourse represented by the explanation of the card game, the historical rationalization and overview, is in intersection with the action language of romantic adventure fiction. The parodic use of these discourses, as I said above, is not primarily satirical; rather, the ideologies that inform and shape those languages are free to come into play and to negotiate with each other. Dove is not interested in gutting an ideology; she wants to discover its narrative life.

The charm and satisfaction that the reader finds in "The Sailor in Africa" stem from the skill with which the two discourses are refracted via the narrative voice: like sirens, the appeal is vicariously to the dream of action and, more cerebrally, to the craving for intellectual order. These contrasting languages *both* speak to us, and in their stylized contiguity there is an almost erotic frisson. This is accentuated by the succession of verse paragraphs that are either suspenseful enjambments drawn out from stanza to stanza or refusals of climax in sudden switches of protagonist and location. Not least of the pleasures for the reader is in observing the knowingness of these tactics that brilliantly, succinctly, combine those of prose fiction and poetry.

The title poem of the fourth part, "Primer for the Nuclear Age," is a reminder that at the edge of such elaborations, beyond our cultural mappings, lurk "Monsters," and that "Any fear, any / memory will do" to set them off. The first line of each of the four short stanzas has a left justification, as if literally testifying to the edge between order and anarchy. In warning of the dangers of having a "heart," the poem is a prelude to "Parsley," which concludes the volume. In "Primer for the Nuclear Age," the "skull" sits comfortably in the pantry, the domestic setting from which evil emanates.

"Parsley" is a sophisticated achievement, not least because it traces the ideological couplings of sophistication and naïveté in the psychology of evil. The poem follows the mental processes of a dictator that led to the mass slaughter of twenty thousand blacks in the Dominican Republic in 1957. It is alleged that Rafael Trujillo ordered their deaths because they could not pronounce the letter *r* in *perejil,* the Spanish word for parsley. Dove seeks to examine the psychopathology of such an individual who directs large-scale atrocities, who seem to be outside the human map. What are the transformations that turn the family man into a mass murderer, the ordinary into the extraordinary?

Dove has spoken of her struggles with the shape of the poem that seemed to require a repetitive driven form, such as a sestina. Although she gave up the idea of adhering precisely to the rigor of the sestina pattern, the vestigial elements of it in the second part are effective. The first part is a villanelle, a well nigh impossible form that consists of a series of tercets concluded by a quatrain, rhymed on two rhymes in an aba formula in the tercets and abaa in the quatrain. The first line of the first tercet is the last line of each even tercet, the last line of the first tercet is the last line of each odd tercet, and the first and third lines of the first tercet are the third and fourth of the quatrain (I give the details with apologies to those readers who retain the scheme of this exacting form in their memory). The scheme is not quite perfectly carried through in "Parsley," but it is very close. Why did Dove choose such a demanding format? She has referred to "the sound cage"[22] of the poem, the acoustic imagery in the repetition of *r* in words such as "parrot" so that the sounds become symbolic of the fixated mindset of the dictator and the predicament of the victims who are compelled "to speak their own death sentences."[23]

The first part of "Parsley," "The Cane Fields," in the form of the villanelle, is from the perspective of the Haitian cane cutters who cannot roll the Spanish *r*, who say "Katalina" rather than Katarina. The repetitions of the poem are also sinister transformations. In the third tercet, the cane cutters, having been cut down themselves, become the cane:

> Like a parrot imitating spring,
>
> we lie down screaming as rain punches through
> and we come up green.

Nature itself seems to have gone awry, to have metamorphosed into assailants, rolling the dead bodies into the earth as fertilization. The natural cycle has turned into a hideous cycle of violence: the general's teeth shining as he laughs are reminiscent of the dragon's teeth that sprang up as a furious army of men in the myth of Jason. Whether as color or sound, parsley is a mocking emanation of evil erupting from within the familiar and of destruction as a hideous parody of the renewal of spring: "For every drop of blood / there is a parrot imitating spring."

The second part of the poem, "The Palace," imaginatively reconstructs, using flashbacks and interior monologue, the festering brew of vindictiveness, sentimentality, and paranoia that ferments into the fateful edict. "It is fall, when thoughts turn / to love and death": the philosophical elevation of these lines in the first stanza ironically undermines the unphilosophical nature of the general's meditations. Arbitrarily, his mother's death as she baked "skull-shaped candies / for the Day of the Dead" becomes linked with the sweet pastries provided for the parrot that fill him with revulsion and bring back the memory of his first killing. From sugar pastries to the sugar cane and the machetes of sugar cane workers and their stupid inability to pronounce the letter *r* as his mother could, the crazy sequence drives him into a frenzy of sentimentality and hatred: the "tear" that "splashes" on his boot conflates with the "mud and urine" splashed on his boots on his first day of battle.

The inexorability and absurdity of this crazed progression is finely dramatized. The general is both a child again sobbing for his mother and a practiced dictator with a childish self-importance: "He will / order many, this time, to be killed." The phrase that Dove uses to describe her preoccupation in *Museum* as a whole, her effort to deal with "anything that becomes frozen by memory, or by circumstance, or by history"[24] is clearly especially applicable to this poem in which a banal conjunction of memory and circumstance sets off the act that becomes frozen in the lens of history. Trujillo's emotional fossilization is obliquely registered in the figural transfers between "teeth" and "arrowheads," images he associates with his mother. The perversity of his act is revealed in his choice of the word "parsley" because he remembers the sprigs of parsley that men wore to symbolize the birth of a son. As a good son honoring his mother, he will be fertile in action: from this "single beautiful word" he will multiply death. The poem abounds with these paradoxes of fecundity and death, with the overflow of the fixated and narcissistic into the "rain" of terror.

In "Parsley," Dove is presenting a "primer" of one of the ways in which individuals get "mean" (to quote from the epigraph to part 4 of *Museum*). The poem is itself almost in danger of becoming a museum piece, a famous exhibit conscientiously viewed by students. As if to preempt such solemnities, "Dusting" was originally placed as the prologue to *Museum*.

It was eventually to become an integral part of the next volume, *Thomas and Beulah* (1986), but initially came "out of nowhere"[25] while writing *Museum*. As Dove said, it does not fit in the body of the collection, but it is an insightful prelude. Its domestic ordinariness stands in contradistinction to the scope of the volume that, even when it touches base on the quotidian, intends to range globally. "Dusting" is an image of reader-response activity; the reader necessarily approaches history intimately yet laboriously:

> Each dust
> stroke a deep breath and
> the canary in bloom.

The phrase "canary in bloom" is thus an image of the lyric propensity of a poem: its "bloom" (in the sense of patina or bloom of dust) will "bloom" (in the sense of flowering) in the "patient" dusting off (the reading), which will reveal the creative "life" of the poem. Any volume of poetry is a mausoleum of the vitality with which it was constructed. It has to be warmed into life, its "ice / dissolved" by the reader. The art of poetry includes the art of reading. This reader-response interpretation is not at all to deny gendered or other readings that the poem invites in *Thomas and Beulah* but to suggest that its placing in relation to *Museum* is self-reflexive about the stasis of art, the paradoxes of its prolonged shelf life.

Indeed, for example, a structuralist unpacking of "Dusting" feeds into the above emphasis on the reader's role. It reveals a pattern of binary oppositions, such as wilderness and promise, death and resurrection, frozen ice and free-flowing water, memory as lock(et) and release. For "Dusting" might be said to be about the ways in which a poem can reflect the flux of memory that *moved* it into being and that then works in mysterious ways with the reader's *work,* "each dust stroke a deep breath," returning the "dark wood," the made object, to life. Readers might prefer a more exalted metaphor for their literary labors, but the image is consonant with the declared aims of the volume, which are to release historical figures and objects from the dust and silt of history and bring them to living speech.

CHAPTER 4

Thomas and Beulah

A Dream Deferred

The extraordinary achievement of *Thomas and Beulah* is not only that it is one of the significant works of American cultural definition in the twentieth century but also that it meets the generic challenges of the long poem, expressing both intimacy and range in its formal elisions and metaphorical virtuosity. The sequence has become well known to critics yet is always a revelation in its combination of bold historical sweep with close focus upon individual identity, the changing landscape of the American dream highlighted in the personal moment. It is a work of considerable historical imagination, of powerful cultural inwardness, of precisely judged distance, and of a sensibility that never presumes on empathy or sanctions sentimentality. As an artistic achievement, the quality of *Thomas and Beulah* has yet to be fully recognized. It has been valued as black history, as family memorial, as gender critique, and as formally innovative. The poem is, of course, all these things. Its artistry lies in their fusion, the tangibility of implicate relationships. It is an artistry that, even as it both locates and universalizes the story of Thomas and Beulah, acknowledges the limitations of its own historicizing procedures.

In the creative evolution of *Thomas and Beulah,* Dove was very conscious of developing and integrating the multiple strands of her enterprise. The book "began as a poem" and then "grew poem by poem,"[1] becoming an extended effort. She wanted to capture the lives of ordinary people caught up in the migration of African Americans from the rural South to the industrialized towns of the North in the early years of the twentieth century. This economic movement, which became known as the Great Migration, had been given pictorial expression in Jacob Lawrence's paintings, the Migration series, first displayed collectively in 1940–41. The series toured American museums in the 1990s, giving the general public an opportunity to visualize and to understand the magnitude of this cultural shift: "[Lawrence] understood that just as slavery had shaped African American life in the nineteenth century, migration would become the defining event in the twentieth."[2] In her interview with Steven Schneider, Dove said of the migration, "It's the first time that blacks in this country had any chance, however stifled, of pursuing 'the American dream.'"[3] Alain LeRoy Locke, the African American visual arts critic who promoted and recommended Jacob Lawrence's series, understood the full significance of the migration:

> Neither labor demand, the boll-weevil nor the Ku Klux Klan is a basic factor, however contributory any or all of them may have been. The wash and rush of this human tide on the beach line of the northern city centers is to be explained primarily in terms of a new vision of a spirit to seize, even in the face of an extortionate and heavy toll, a chance for the improvement of conditions. With each successive wave of it, the movement of the Negro migrant becomes more and more like that of the European waves at their crests, a mass movement toward the larger and more democratic chance—in the Negro's case a deliberate flight not only from countryside to city, but from medieval America to modern.[4]

The period covered in *Thomas and Beulah* is from 1919, when Thomas leaves Tennessee, through his arrival in Akron, Ohio, in 1921, his marriage to Beulah, their years together through the Depression of the thirties, the Second World War, the civil rights movement, until the death of Thomas in 1963 and of Beulah in 1969. *Thomas and Beulah* is a double sequence: the first, *Mandolin,* consists of twenty-three poems for Thomas, and the second, *Canary in Bloom,* is twenty-one poems for Beulah. Written in the third person, both sequences include free, indirect discourse or quoted monologue to register the protagonists' sense of identity, which is woven into omniscient narrative comment. Dove has spoken of the advantage of using the third person perspective as giving "a wider portal to step through."[5] Her explanatory preface, "These poems tell two sides of a story," indicates both a respect for their distinct individuality and an understanding that all marriages encompass separateness, different ways of perceiving, as well as shared experience. The "two sides" are also indicative of the different cultural constraints that marriage involved for men and women in those years. Loosely based upon the experience of her grandparents, Dove was careful from the outset to give herself room for imaginative manoeuver (changing the name of her grandmother from Georgianna to Beulah, for example) in drawing upon family history:

I was after the essence of my grandparents' existence and their survival, not necessarily the facts of their survival. That's the distinction I'm trying to make. So when I said it became less and less about them, I meant I was not so concerned about whether Thomas in the book was born the same year as my grandfather (he wasn't, incidently) or whether in fact it was a yellow scarf he gave Beulah or not.

What's important is the gesture of that scarf. One appropriates certain gestures from the factual life to reinforce a larger sense of truth that is not, strictly speaking, reality.[6]

Thus, although she undertook considerable research into the experience of her own family and into the history of African Americans in Akron during this period, she was not constrained by documentation and, indeed, chose a form that would counteract and check the causal momentum of narrative. The power of the poem lies in the tension between temporal continuity and disjunct episodes taken out of time. The formal choices that Dove made were designed to use that tension creatively:

I thought there must be a way to get back into poetry the grandness that narrative can give, plus the sweep of time. Lyric poetry does not have that sweep of time. Lyrics are discrete moments. On the other hand, a lot of narrative poems tend to bog down in the prosier transitional moments. I didn't see very many long narrative poems that really weren't smaller poems linked together. So one of the things I was trying to do was string moments as beads on a necklace. In other words, I have lyric poems which, when placed one after the other, reconstruct the sweep of time. I wanted it all. I wanted a narrative and I wanted lyric poems, so I tried to do them both.[7]

What is interesting here is the language of Dove's analogy in that she finds a way both to roughen, to make salient, and to *reconcile* lyric and narrative, so that although, on the one hand, her method is the fragment, formally disjunctive and elliptical, on the other hand, the overall sweep of the poem threads motif to motif into an enhancing musical harmony. This obviously has features of the geometry of classical musical structure, but equally, it refers to the looser, more evasive patterns of black music. Lynn Keller, in identifying Dove's handling of the long poem, has quoted Lawrence Levine's description of black folk song to mark characteristic features that are incorporated in *Thomas and Beulah*: "The structural units in Negro folksongs are typically the metaphor and line rather than the plot; Negro songs don't tend to weave narrative elements together to create a story but instead accumulate images to create a feeling."[8]

Dove does craft her work by an internal self-referentiality in the modernist sense, accruing symbolic resonance by image repetition, and she does forego certain kinds of narrative connection. It is evident, however, when studying her formal patterning in detail, that it is markedly eclectic and cannot be tied to any one formal source. Catholic in enterprise, she brings different forms of organization into the equation. Thus the forty-four poems of this long poem sequence cannot be fully understood without recourse to the appended chronology, as if to admit the claims of this more conventional sequencing. The chronology itself mixes the dates of important events in the lives of Thomas and Beulah with public events, an affirmation of the value of the lives of ordinary people, "these nobodies in the course of history"[9] as Dove referred to them. In my detailed discussion of *Thomas and Beulah* below, beginning with the *Mandolin* sequence, I shall try to convey how the formal patterning is an expression of a complex cultural and historical engagement that entails a correspondingly composite aesthetic.

Mandolin

Music, the mandolin, is integral to Thomas's story. The first three poems cover the beginning of his journey north from Tennessee with Lem, his inseparable friend, the tragic "event" that marks his whole life, and his arrival alone in Akron, Ohio, in 1921. In the opening poem, "The Event," Lem's ready response to Thomas daring him to swim out to "a tree-capped island" on the river is characteristic of their high spirits, but this audacity is disrupted by a lurch of fortune: Lem drowns and Thomas, standing helplessly on deck,

> saw the green crown shake
> as the island slipped
>
> under, dissolved
> in the thickening stream.
> At his feet
>
> a stinking circle of rags,
> the half-shell mandolin.[10]

The precise lineation and the exactitude of the enjambment trace how this heart-wrenching moment is emotionally etched into Thomas's psyche. The American dream, the "green breast of the new world," momentarily possible for the two young black men, as it was for "the Dutch sailors"[11] recalled at the end of *The Great Gatsby,* is reached for but slips and is gone. The musicality of the transition from the jaunty churning of the river boat to the elegaic water shirring over Lem's grave as the "green crown" is lost, condenses and intensifies the loss. The Great Migration of such historical moment in twentieth-century American culture is conceived here specifically in terms of individual destiny. The shape of the mandolin, associated now with guilt and emptiness, is symbolic of Thomas as a "half-shell" survivor. It is ironic that this "event" is not in the appended chronology: the significant markers of the inner life are not of the kind to be documented.

The second poem, "Variation on Pain," is based on a complex analogy between the structure of the instrument, the relationship between Lem and Thomas, and the shape of pain: "Two strings, one pierced cry." A mandolin string seems to be "Like a rope stretched clear / To land," both mocking and consolatory, yet also, a heart-string, a "man gurgling air," a too nearly human struggling sound. The play or variation upon the meaning of "lobe" as the fleshly vestigial one that remains of a fissured two, as the literally pierced earlobe, and as the emotionally harrowing sound of the mandolin that imitates Lem's death cry, links an abstraction, a quotidian detail, and the traumatized response of the survivor. What remains is the understanding that death has joined the two men indissolubly.

What Thomas becomes from this point onward derives from their psychic inseparability, a debt of pain that ultimately makes it possible for the past to be "forgiven." Yet this inner seal of relationship carries with it an external dislocation, a loss of ease, as Thomas, the survivor, struggles to make a life for himself, to create a viable identity, his "life a perpetual scramble toward definition."[12] His jaunty persona in the third poem, "Jiving," is a fragile construct, a paradoxical self-creation. There is both a brash adoption of Lem's old swagger in learning to play the mandolin and a pushing back of the tragedy into "another's life," as if it had happened to someone else. The poem opens with a colloquial assurance, "Heading North," but the exchange of the old "river-bright" Tennessee landscape for the "dingy," industrial Akron is premonitory of the difficulties ahead, and Thomas's peacock colors and frenetic strumming are compensatory, overcompensatory. Earlobes pierced now by flashy jewelry, he is a stereotype of the folksy good-time charmer:

> The young ladies
> saying *He sure plays*
>
> *that tater bug*
> *like the devil!*
>
> sighing their sighs
> and dimpling.

The juxtapositions of the three opening poems, elliptical and lyrical in their rendering of shifts in mood and fortune, of identity shaped by circumstance and by Keatsian provings of the heart, have also grandeur in their cultural sweep, the registering of exodus, loss, and reorientation. The new world seems within grasp but becomes a treacherous mirage sucking idealism into its wake, leaving the survivor to internalize its lessons as painful memory, the reaching out already "borne back ceaselessly into the past."[13] The insouciance of outsetting in the first poem so soon becomes caricature minstrelsy in the third, which, in turn, becomes the straw man diminished by the reality of industrial labor in the fourth.

This is a narrative of more than the temporary discouragements of one man, however. The intersections of language between the three poems compress the intersections of history and geography in their transitions: the "Tennessee ridge" of the first poem (where Lem and Thomas were raised) becomes the "ridged sound" of the mandolin in the second, as if landscape and culture become simultaneously and contrastingly both emblem of scar tissue (the sign of the wound) and, more positively, something carried as internalized strength. The mandolin is an intimate and portable version of the South, a cultural signifier of the migrant black male, its tactile "geography" of shape, surface, and texture the map of pain. The Tennessee landscape, the human body and the instrument are implicate, bonded, not to be disentangled. The title of the poem "Variation on Pain" suggests a formal musical analogy for Thomas's individual guilt and anguish, but it is also a cultural variation, just another hard-luck story in the ups and downs of the movement north.

The fourth poem, "Straw Hat," expresses the anonymity and degrading conditions of labor that young male migrants found in the North. The longer stanzas, unlike the street-jive couplets of the preceding poem, register stagnation. The "narrow grief" of shift work has replaced the Whitmanesque freedoms of the past, when Thomas "lay on / so many kinds of grass." Jacob Lawrence's paintings numbered forty-seven and forty-eight in the Migration series show the cell-like barracks in which migrants slept, with iron bedsteads dominating the pictorial space like prison bars. Thomas, in spite of such conditions, retains something of his folksy southern gallantry in casual sexual encounters; the tipping of his straw hat is an emblem of courtesy. Music, however, is only spreading the pain; it is not a consolation or resource. The questioning epigraph to *Mandolin* from Melvin B. Tolson, "Black Boy, O Black Boy, / is the port worth the cruise?" (which picks up the demeaning epithet for the adult black male used by whites), seems especially pertinent to Thomas's disoriented existence after his arrival in Akron.

Integration comes, paradoxically and conventionally, via the uncertainties of romantic love in "Courtship." The poem highlights two discrete moments. In the first, the resplendent Thomas, ever the dandy in his "yellow scarf" and "houndstooth vest," asks Beulah for a date (she is not, in fact, named in this poem or in any other throughout the *Mandolin* sequence).

The second moment is the scene of asking her father's permission for their marriage in a "parlor festooned / like a ship" (one of the many plays on the literal meaning of "courtship" in the sequence). These are clearly high events of personal history liable to be sanctified and congealed in the memory of the participants, the "photo album" mode as John Shoptaw has noted.[14] It also signals Thomas's entrance into the consumer good life. Coincident with caring for someone else is the ability to perform the gesture of putting his expensive yellow scarf round his fiancée's shoulders: "(He made / good money; he could buy another.)." But the mixture of motives in the still vain but self-made owner of a "turtledove Nash" is the potent combination that gives him self-worth. This is clear from the "mandolin belly pressed tight" to his chest, as if part of his fragile substantiality. There is an irony, though, in that the man who has so often played his "*tater bug*" as an instrument of seduction now feels himself subservient to the courtship ideology, "selling all for a song," giving up his freedom in the most hackneyed way. If Thomas is rueful about this, the closing lines of the poem affirm the emotional vulnerability and necessity of the occasion for personal fulfilment: "His heart fluttering shut / then slowly opening." The artistry of this poem is in the synecdochic[15] cultural touches that express the transitions of the love affair. Beulah's pleated skirt is first a "circlet of arrows," a fan of cupid's darts, softly provocative and piercing; then later, as they dance, Thomas "flicks" the now responsively "sighing" pleats. The sway of love is rendered in all its intimacy and cultural predictability.

The language of love, as Roland Barthes has remarked in *A Lover's Discourse*, is culturally assigned a peculiar, unreal, private status, "exiled from all gregarity,"[16] yet it is ubiquitous, used, reused, flagrantly public and second-hand in song and thus oxymoronic, an intimate banality. Dove is unerring in those Barthesian indices of culture as nature, the expression of "a lover's discourse" as a "great stream of the Image-repertoire,"[17] a discourse "spoken by thousands" yet also somehow exiled to "the unreal."[18] Her songlike rhymes "in the spirit of country blues"[19] as a formal element within the lyric poem "Refrain" (which follows "Courtship") are a recognition of how this discourse threads our lives, heartstring internalized from the cultural foam of language. The sophistication of perspective, the eye for the mythological apparatus of culture accentuates, by contrast, the enthusiasms of young love: "*Count your kisses / Sweet as honey*" is the refrain to the oak bed "pitching / with its crew, / a man and a wife." The poem mixes coarse and smooth, banana and silk, commerce and copulation with Rabelaisian gusto. The buoyant opening, with the ship metaphor still in play, a nursery rhyme recharged, in which the mandolin becomes the crescent moon, is humorous and tender. The honeymoon freedom in midwestern, urban Akron, Ohio, seems momentarily not unlike the southern myths of raft and river freedoms. Yet Thomas is still the man who carries within his northern self his southern tragedy. The glancing references to rags and drunkenness at the moment of sexual ecstasy recall Lem's death, and the poem ends with an italicized nostalgic lyric of pastoral innocence, an ambiguous and potent signifier reminiscent of Lem and of an Edenic existence the carelessness of which is, for Thomas, retrospectively shadowed by guilt. The title "Refrain" has both a simple robust exuberance and a complexity of feeling backed up from the past.

Such links are evident in the title of the poem in which Thomas awaits the birth of his first child. "Variation on Guilt" recalls the earlier "Variation on Pain," and the word "Count" picks up a refrain from the previous poem with a more urgent sense of being accountable for rather than amassing. Thomas is again the "bystander," the helpless male chagrined by the arrival of a girl, comically outmaneuvered by feminine mystique yet aware of his own entrapment in gender rituals. The play on words such as "deal" and "count," with their clichéd echoes of card playing or tags such as "count your blessings," "count me out" or "in," has an idiomatic finesse. Thomas "deals the cigars" inwardly raging at the poor hand of having been dealt a girl.

The poem that follows, "Nothing Down," is an ironic play on Thomas's sense of buying into, but somehow being sold short on, the American dream. As he and his wife choose a new car to pay by installments for a return trip to Tennessee, he is aware of all the bad things that he and Lem had planned to escape. Yet he is also haunted by the family closeness, the wilderness freedoms of his childhood. The italicized sections of the poem are fragments of the past, the bitter paradoxes of southern black existence that continue to undermine his belief in himself or his sense that he has found something better. Even his adult desire for a "sky blue Chandler" is predicated on a boyhood narrow escape from being hunted down and lynched. The blue flower in the woods was a refuge from brutality and an emblem of separateness from human fear. Thomas feels locked into these traumatic memories and is still living in a racist culture, subject to racist abuse by whites, when the newly purchased car breaks down. It is as if color can never be an unalloyed aesthetic pleasure for him, not a *"blue trumpet of Heaven"* but inextricably linked with shame and humiliation, an inescapable template of consciousness.

The building of the Goodyear Zeppelin Air-Dock in Akron in 1929 was one of the symbols of innovation and commercial success that, in retrospect, seem like the bubble that was to be deflated in the Depression of the thirties. Assembly-line labor in itself swallows up humanity. The ninth poem, "The Zeppelin Factory," is the first of a somber series detailing Thomas's loss of confidence in those difficult years. The huge span of the Zeppelin building is a "whale's belly" with Thomas laboring within it as an afflicted Jonah. The disaster of the airship *Akron* in 1931, in which a man fell to his death, strikes at his imagination:

> *Here I am, intact*
> *and faint-hearted.*

Guiltily reminded of Lem's death, he feels unfit to be a survivor. The threat of union violence as the Depression takes hold is registered in the poem "Under the Viaduct, 1932." Thomas, unemployed and with a growing family, is withdrawn, vengeful, and brooding. The colors of the poem are death colors, the snow a winding sheet. There is no mandolin.

The next three poems, each very different in form, are poems of recovery, of what might be called Thomas's maturity, although with all the recognitions of frustration, adjustment, and bewilderment that maturity involves. The first, "Lightnin' Blues,"[20] has Thomas struggling to reconcile the roles of Friday night blues player, expert fisherman, and weekend husband taking his family out for a drive, kids bickering in the back seat and everything going wrong. Listening to "a canary" (Billie Holiday) on the radio as he struggles to drive through a thunderstorm, the car breaks down, which turns out to be a miraculous piece of luck saving the family from a fallen tree on the road. The poem wittily adjudicates between "canary" and "Kingfish," between feminine priorities and plaints and masculine pleasures and pursuits.

The taming of Thomas, but also his further humanizing, is pithily encapsulated in the poem "Compendium":

> He gave up fine cordials and
> his hounds-tooth vest.
>
> He became a sweet tenor
> in the gospel choir.

This is the emergence of the family man, envious of the way his wife's canary usurps her affections, resigned father of four girls neatly boxed in their bedroom, but a man whose mandolin hangs on the wall, who has had to give up fancy clothes. The sum of the gains and losses of family life is succinctly set out. A static résumé, however, is only one way of looking at Thomas's life, and the poem on the facing page, "Definition in the Face of Unnamed Fury," expresses the resentments of marriage with comic verve.[21] Thomas rails against "That dragonfly," the yellow silk scarf of his courting days that hangs faded on the wall, and even more furiously against the canary, "that sun-bleached delicacy / in its house of sticks." The mandolin becomes an instrument of querulous self-pitying complaint, of sexual frustration. There is Thomas the conforming family man, but there is also Thomas the bitter rager against the dying of the light.

The two poems of the period of the Second World War, "Aircraft" and "Aurora Borealis," show Thomas as a shrunken figure: his masculine frustrations within the family are intensified in the workplace. "Too frail for combat," he works at Goodyear

Aircraft alongside women. The central metaphor of the poem, the invisible wing of the spirit as implicit contrast to the repetitive assembly line labor of constructing the aircraft wing, is redolent of the mythical Daedalus, the fabulous artificer whose goal was "flying toward the sun." But it is an ironic analogy in the light of Thomas's sense of impotence, as is the riveting gun with which he works. The assembly line, although not combat, is essential war work, yet even here Thomas feels inferior, relegated to the aircraft wing as more crude clumsy work than that of the women who "dabble" with deft hands in the "gnarled intelligence" of the engine. The condensed, intricate form of "Aircraft" has been brilliantly explicated by Helen Vendler.[22] The poem is also a succinct historical marker in which the experience of a representative individual is isolated and made salient. The ordinary destiny is momentarily caught in the glare of the lens of history, poignantly outlined against the backdrop of the huge forces of energy that comprise war.

In "Aurora Borealis," the reversal of the fortunes of war as the Americans began to turn the tables in the Pacific and dropped atomic bombs on Japan in 1945 seems to the weary aircraft workers of Akron who watch the newsreel to prefigure the end of the war. The "Aurora Borealis" flickering on the cinema screen is not the northern lights but the "crippling radiance" of Hiroshima. For Thomas, the collective relief is stained by personal memory. With the intensified guilt of the survivor, he is drawn back into the nightmare of Lem's tragedy. As he emerges from the cinema, the blackness of the night sky becomes, in his mind, the darkness of the river water in which he *himself* is now drowning. The poet, distinct from her protagonist, observes a decorum of scale: the atomic "veil" suspended in the sky is beyond individual human capacity to mourn. In this scale of happening, Thomas must be returned to a domestic, a manageable context:

> So much

> For despair.
> Thomas, go home.

This poem and the preceding one touch on the ordinary feelings of wartime industrial workers, confused recipients of newsreel ideology, those who were needed but were not heroes, for men a feeling of emasculation and redundancy. The psychic blight of war, the failure of the follow-through from spirit to action, is evident in the negativizing of the imagery of light in the poems.

The poem-sequence of *Mandolin,* structured as it is, like a musical sequence with variation, represents the tonalities of the individual and collective psyche not only in musical terms but also in terms of color. "Aurora Borealis," with its reversals and confusions of the significance of the patterns of nature, of sky and water, of past and future, is a chiaroscuro of light and dark in which the "radiance" of Hiroshima is a deadly light, darker than the dark of war.

However, Thomas's own sense of desolation is followed by a saving recovery of spirit in the succeeding poem, "Variation on Gaining a Son." The memories of Lem's death, the feelings of masculine isolation are miraculously overlaid with pleasure when, at his daughter's wedding in 1945, Thomas discovers a fellow-feeling for his soldier son-in-law. In the love and war between the sexes, they are comrades. Family continuity, the generations "drilled neatly" into the ideology of courtship and marriage, is a matrix of feeling in which Thomas is ironically yet tenderly enfolded.

It is also from this point in the sequence, as in any personal life cycle, that Thomas, in acknowledging the new adult generation, steps to the sidelines of his own life, his consciousness now accepting memory, the past as its most significantly active feature. The title of the next poem, "One Volume Missing," suggests the written record of his life with Lem's death as a significant shaping absence. But Thomas is now more able to accept the surge of memory. The cover of an encyclopedia that he buys in the church rummage sale returns him to the tragic drowning, but also to the "slow afternoons" of childhood innocence. The last volume of the encyclopedia is missing, which is in one way a bonus: "no wars." The poem's visual layout modulates from the ellipses of the opening stanza to the enjambed rendering of the elastic reach of memory in the long single line "slow afternoons with a line and a bent nail," which holds the childhood pastoral poignantly in suspension. The effect is to stretch out toward "here," the man who suffered standing before the "interrupted wing" in the aircraft factory but whose spirit, like that of Dedalus, still hungers toward knowledge. Meditative and cryptic, allusive in reflecting on so many other poems in the *Mandolin* sequence, the poem is bleak in the notation of the shabbiness and exclusions of Thomas's life. Yet it is also comforting in that his life takes on the mysterious shapings and refigurings of memory, the swirling and blotching in which the coalescings of nature, culture and spirit, can be discerned, momentously. It is as if the cheap encyclopedia becomes, momentarily, the Book of Life.

The last volume of Thomas's life is "missing" in that it is yet to be fulfilled. The final poems of the sequence are imbued with his sense of life drawing to a close, which both licenses and eases his revisiting of the past. For *Mandolin* is not only *about* him but is his autobiography, and as his life comes to the full, he meditates more deliberately on its shaping events and does not try to push them away into "another's life" as in the early poem "Jiving." His life has been both a charmed one, endowed by Lem, and a haunted one, which in his darker dreams he knows to have been fortuitously and undeservedly given. The title of the poem "The Charm" indicates both the haunting and the lucky element of his life. The ghostly twin that haunts his nightmares in "The Charm," however, is complemented by the sense of community in the poem "Gospel," with its inspirational surge from "Swing Low Sweet Chariot":

> *Swing low so I*
> *can step inside—*
> a humming ship of voices
>
> . . . .
> No sound this generous
> could fail:

The "humming ship" that holds Thomas steady, which contains and expresses wrong and can "ride joy," buoyed up by water, is here not the medium of drowning but of salvation. The gospel music idiom carries the poem thrillingly and seductively: the short lines of the quatrains cut and shape while the enjambment slithers and escapes histrionically. In a loving vibrato of cold and hot, stanza and syntax, like tenor and contralto, high and low, create an ongoing pattern in which Thomas "swims homeward warbling." If the mandolin is the instrument of isolated lyric pain, the gospel choir shares, elaborates, and cathartically chases pain heavenward.

Thomas has other communal ways of giving narrative shape to his life in telling stories about his childhood to his grandchildren:

as oral historian, allowing himself appropriate embellishments, in response to the audience expectations. The poem "Roast Possum" is nostalgic anecdote, a tall tale of his childhood in Wartrace, Tennessee. But it is also an authentic telling that counteracts the information about the characteristics of the Negro (which Thomas does not relay to his grandchildren) in the 1909 Werner Encyclopedia. The poem has a more leisurely narrative sprawl, as if allowing space for embellishment; "*old-time know-how*" is both a fiction in the poem and a survival skill, like playing possum, which he knows his grandchildren will need. With his literally minded grandson, too, Thomas can play out, "man to man," pleasurable fictions of masculinity. The juxtaposition of "Gospel" and "Roast Possum" links, in a benignly comic spirit, the fundamental ways in which personal experience is narrativized, joined together with other lives in a healing way. In this portrayal, Dove is very much concerned with "the underside of the story" affirming the importance of these ordinary moments in "shaping our concept of ourselves."[23]

The final three poems of the *Mandolin* sequence, "The Stroke," the harbinger of the end, "The Satisfaction Coal Company," in which Thomas in retirement thinks back to the time in the thirties when he had a part-time janitor's job, and "Thomas at the Wheel," the heart failure that kills him, are an unsentimentalized presentation of old age. They are expressed in large part from Thomas's own perspective. The narrative mode modulates between his retelling of the experiences to others and his own interior consciousness of the events. In "The Stroke," he tells the experience in different ways at different times, jokingly or fearfully as his mood and the occasion demands. The mental confusions or disorientations of his condition in the aftermath of the stroke are represented not as a disability but as an inner secret,

an intense return to early experiences of his marriage in which
"the sun shone like the summer / in which she was pregnant
with their first," as if the inner landscape is intensely irradiated.
In the final stanza of the poem, Thomas recognizes that it is Lem
beckoning him:

> he knows it was Lem all along:
> Lem's knuckles tapping his chest in passing,
> Lem's heart, for safekeeping,
> he shores up in his arms.

Thomas's sense that his whole life has been lived for Lem, as
guardian of Lem's spirit, is expressed with great poignancy in
this closing metaphor. He "shores up" the heart of his drowned
comrade in his own frail heart, and his death will be a reunion
recognizing his own life as a debt owed. The language has a
Shakespearian assurance in its expansion from the colloquial to
the fullness of emotion in the compass of four lines.

Retirement has yet to exact its full range of ennui for Thomas
before the end comes. The satiric title of "The Satisfaction Coal
Company" signals its ironic tenor. Two phases of Thomas's life
are compared. His memories of the struggles of the Depression
when sweeping floors for a coal company at least gave him
warmth and the opportunity to take coal home for his family,
whereas now, in retirement, the "gas heater takes care of itself"
so that he does not have much to do in providing for basic
needs. His problem is more "What to do with a day," and his
return in memory to the difficult year of 1934 is as if to comfort
himself imaginatively in recalling that intensity of need and of
being needed.

The title of the final poem, "Thomas at the Wheel," is ironic
in that his life, lived through the Depression and two world wars,

through years of racial inequality and through large scale industrial transitions, has not been one in which he could ever confidently have felt in command. Even his youthful act of self-assertion and choice in migrating north was marked by tragedy. Yet he is a man who has weathered these things, and it is not accidental that the automobile and the weather are the setting for his final scene. He traveled north for a better life materially, and he has in some part found it. He has found the "neon script," the commercialism of the consumer life, and he has made the adjustments and acquired the nostalgias that such an upheaval of identity entails. The poem opens with Thomas's final collapse:

> This, then, the river he had to swim.
> Through the wipers the drugstore
> shouted, lit up like a casino,
> neon script leering from the shuddering asphalt.

The opening line, "This, then, the river he had to swim," is imbued not only with the past, with Lem's drowning and the sense of cyclical return to his friend, but also with resolution in the face of death. The classical resonance of the underworld crossing of the Styx gives dignity to Thomas's plight, trapped in his automobile unable to move to get help: the exterior deluge "emptying" ironically contrasts with his own chest "filling with water." His last thought is a joke to himself about the symbolism of water in his own life: the death of Belshazzar, the king of Babylon, as narrated in Daniel 5, was prefigured by a mysterious hand writing on the wall; Thomas's death is written in water on the windshield.

That the experience is refracted through Thomas's consciousness is a kind of control. His own awareness of his condition and helplessness is stoic. He notes the detachments of urban living, the man who comes out of the drugstore and looks him "calmly in the eye" at the moment when death is prizing him from life. The conclusion of the poem is masterly:

> He lay down across
> the seat, a pod set to sea,
> a kiss unpuckering. He watched
> the slit eye of the glove compartment,
> the prescription inside,
>
> he laughed as he thought *Oh*
> *the writing on the water.*

The "slit eye" of the glove compartment that holds his prescription has the kind of precise objectivity that generates the terminal claustrophobia of an Emily Dickinson poem, but with a difference in that Dove holds the Gothic potential of such an image in check. The fact that death comes at a moment of being alone and helpless is structurally rather than emotively rendered by images that provide a visual equivalence of the compressed stages of shock and submission: first the panic, the "neon script leering," and then the "slit eye," both recording observer and an external equivalent of his own eye closing in death, and then, finally, the emergency sirens, the human world of panic and trauma continuing as Thomas fades from it, the car keys "ticking" after his own heart has stopped. It is significant that the first two images mirror Thomas's deteriorating bodily state. The final image of keys positions him at the moment of transition from his earthly and American quest for a better material life, which the keys to the car represent, to the question of his meeting with St. Peter, his entrance to the kingdom of heaven. The classical and biblical resonances are self-ironizing, jocular, and discreet rather than portentous, taking their place without affectation alongside the homely images of Thomas as lover, "kiss unpuckering," or seed-bearer, a "pod set to sea," his place in nature accomplished and generative. There is a sense, too, in which he *is* "at the wheel." Thomas's ordinary death alone on a city street gathers meaning, the lines steadying as, in his own mind, he shapes and adds this "event" to the other that began his story and then narrates himself out of his own existence, thinking of his wife missing him as he gives himself over to the continuity of memory.

And, indeed, family memory and a granddaughter's determination to recover the "essence" of Thomas's existence have given his story "a larger sense of truth"[24] that is not just a documentary integrity. Dove's narration throughout the sequence has been deferential to the wellsprings of the interior life. Her search for ways in which history can attain the imaginative authority of autobiography is encoded in the text. In the first poem, "The Event," the archaic verb "dove" is used to figure Lem's vitality but also used as a pun on her own name, as if the feat of historical recovery must be both active and deep. For Lem is a figure of lost narratives and of a human spirit cherished and recovered in the imagination. It is notable that, in fact, Dove did have to *imagine* Lem because as she said in an interview, "I knew nothing about the man. My grandfather never mentioned the story to us as children."[25]

There is self-reflexivity, too, in the understanding that to represent any life is to shape biographically what has also been pondered autobiographically. Thomas is convincingly portrayed as one who reflects upon his own life. Looking in the water, his temptation is self-contempt. In Blakean terms, experience has negatively muddied the clear glass of his innocent childhood. Subject to low self-esteem rather than narcissistic self-love, he is at once prosaic and romantic in his struggle for self-worth. Getting by and getting on as he can, he has an interior life of symbol and irony. Dove's historicizing imagination, in expressing that inner life with such attention to its own symbol making, and in linking the representative lives of the two men so profoundly in the imagination of Thomas, the survivor, draws out the depth and complexity of his spirit. The art of *Mandolin* is that it is *his* story as much as it is cultural history. The musical instrument is an image of Thomas's spirit and shaping, as it is also an image of how it is to be recovered and played.

Canary in Bloom

The title of Beulah's sequence, *Canary in Bloom,* the caged bird that is such an irritation to Thomas as a rival to his wife's affections, obviously has a more domestic focus than a mandolin, symbol of a traveling man. Beulah's life is represented as more inwardly lived and restricted than Thomas's;[26] her dreams are fantasies based on certain kinds of deprivation and unfulfillment. *Canary in Bloom* suggests blooming, but it is an ambiguous term also indicative of bloom as the cloud on a polished surface that Beulah encounters when dusting. The masculine and feminine roles that marriage assigns allot them markedly separate spheres of activity, and hers is more conditioned to obedience and self-limitation than his. There is no sense in which she feels able to pursue the American dream for herself, and there is irony in the fact that her fantasies are projected onto ancien régime France.

The first poem, "Taking in Wash," sets the note of women accommodating to and working around the vagaries of men but also having to be resolute and strong. Beulah's father's moods are like the weather. Drunk, ruinous to the laundry, he is something to be put up with. At other times, adoring, playful in an "arctic of sheets," he is potentially dangerous to a pubescent daughter.[27] Her mother is the moral center of the family. The second poem, "Magic," reveals how Beulah's artistic tendencies find expression in the "rehearsed deception" of magic and in dreams of visiting Paris after seeing a picture of the Eiffel Tower. Her capacity to become so absorbed in a task that she cuts herself without realizing is an ironic parallel to the shepherdess play acting of Marie Antoinette whose fantasies led her to the scaffold. The modern American danger for Beulah is the racist violence of the Klan figured in the "scaffolding strung in lights" that she wakes to one night. The images that link the lives of Marie Antoinette and Beulah in the sequence are not ironic in one direction only. They do more than point a contrast in terms of wealth and status that exposes the delusory nature of Beulah's fantasy. After all, a privileged life did not protect the queen from a violent death, whereas Beulah lives to old age. More poignantly, they are linked by their artistic potential, but both are, in different ways, denied the conditions that would have given them creative discipline rather than the frustrations of compensatory fantasy.

The French mode as a desired life-style is evident in the pun in the title of the third poem, "Courtship, Diligence," in which Thomas's energetic courting is not, to Beulah's mind, as romantic as a Frenchman in a carriage. In fact, she is critical of his performance throughout as vulgar and cheap, ridiculing his mandolin as "Cigar-box music." Thomas's dazed state of mind in the "Courtship" poem in *Mandolin* contrasts comically with Beulah's fastidiousness. The discrepancies between their social interactions and their secret thoughts are not a measure of their hypocrisy but a safety valve for the imagination constructing an ideally gendered world. Beulah has her father as an example of the imperfections of husbands and thus has few illusions about the behavior of men in the practicalities of marriage, so it is not surprising that she should be imaginatively exacting in the courtship phase. The poem of her wedding day, "Promises," is more focused on her indignation at her father's presuming to give advice that he has himself never remotely followed than it is on Thomas, and the final stanza of the poem captures her change of status as she throws her bouquet after the ceremony to the awaiting "meadow of virgins." Beulah has thus internalized a romantic fantasy of aristocratic life that in no way undercuts her everyday assessment of the fallibilities of men.[28]

Married life for Beulah is a life of domestic service both outside and inside her own home. The poem "Dusting" renders the painstaking outward routine of her existence and her inward dependence upon memory and imagination as a solace to the spirit. "From this point on," Robert McDowell has observed, "Beulah's story seeks the form, the shape, of meditation."[29] Just as she dusts the objects with great care, so does she dust down her memories of teenage romance: it is a "grainstorm," a fertile germination of the spirit, an active "joy" in Wordsworthian terms. This is a poem of transference, from present confinement to the freedom of the past, from the claustrophobia of the room to the "rage of light," as if Beulah both gives her life to the "dark wood" of the objects and is energized in spirit by the meticulousness of that labor. Nature is imprisoned and reduced: the first reference to the "wilderness" is indicative of Beulah's plight, and it is also a wilderness of "knicknacks," of the seemingly futile repetition of labor. Yet in the transference between her actions and her interior life, each is imbued with something of the quality of the other: "Each dust / stroke a deep breath," as if she endows the "scrolls and "crests" that she dusts with imaginative value, just as she takes satisfaction in remembering the French-sounding name "Maurice," which triumphantly concludes the poem. The patience and expenditure of physical energy becomes, paradoxically, a saving expenditure, fed into the intensity of her inner life.

It is not, however, as if Beulah's martyrdom in the solarium is represented as some kind of trial that she can pass beyond. The meanings of her name, "Marriage," "Promise" and "Desert-in-Peace," remain significant throughout her life: the dream of betterment and the patience in the face of hardship coexist until her last illness. But being wrapped up in her own thoughts insulates her from the worst stresses and hardships of the twenties and thirties that fall on Thomas as the main provider. The external world is always to some extent dreamlike, at one remove, for Beulah. In "A Hill of Beans," a circus passes by. She feeds the hobos who ride the railroad at her kitchen door; it is a kind of passing show. Meanwhile, Thomas was sleeplessly anxious, "as if at sea."

Pregnancy is a further opportunity to dream alone, to nest domestically. In "Weathering Out," the pregnant Beulah goes with Thomas to see the new Zeppelin Air-Dock. She relates the Zeppelin to her own condition, "large and placid, a lake," floating through, centered on the coming child, whereas Thomas returns from work every evening nearly in tears. Hers is a more cocooned, more sensory existence. The title of the poem "Weathering Out" comes to mean not only getting by but also being attuned to the natural cycle. Beulah is like a large ship weathering the economic storm with insouciance, in contrast to Thomas, buffeted, all "at sea."

Beulah's life is family and neighborhood centered. Dove's grace of spirit in rendering this life without imposing on it a obviously feminist retrospective agenda of deprivation is evident in "The House on Bishop Street." Throughout her work, Dove is preoccupied with defined space, the shelter of house and neighborhood, and their analogies with the house of language and the interior space of the mind. In "House and Yard," part of her lecture "Stepping Out: The Poet in the World," she writes appreciatively of Gaston Bachelard's theoretical constructions of occupied space.[30] As a poet, Dove is intrigued by the ways in which the imagination inhabits defined spaces within a house, differentiates between outside and inside, and creates zones of comfort and security. This fundamental human impulse is evident in Beulah's imaginings of her house and neighborhood. This is in accord with Bachelard, yet there is another creative affinity. The art of conveying the pleasure and satisfaction of domestic arrangements was preeminently the art of Dickens, and Dove has something of that comic largeness of spirit that cherishes the domestic with tender realism, sympathetic to the blooming of the human imagination in unprepossessing circumstances, as in the opening of the poem:

> No front yard to speak of,
> just a porch cantilevered on faith
> where she arranged the canary's cage.

Beulah takes pleasure in passersby praising her canary's song, and she has a picture of a ship in the house, both reminders of the limits of her own existence and the fact that she still yearns for a fuller life: leaning out from her porch, "she could glimpse / the faintest of mauve."

As her children increase, Beulah's need for psychological space becomes more urgent. Even the house itself is something to escape in the poem "Daystar," in which she takes a chair out behind the garage while the children nap, cherishing the time in the middle of the day when she can be "pure nothing." She holds on to the "palace" of her daydreams at night, when "Thomas rolled over and / lurched into her." "Obedience" is a poem that accords Beulah some imaginative space and authority. As she ages, her body slackens, obedient to time, but her imagination becomes more imperative, able to "think up a twilight" or scoff at the "puny stars." The most powerful metaphor of the poem, however, is the concluding one in which she, and her family, become a small but vital part within a larger creative pattern and a longer time span:

> The house shut up like a pocket watch,
> those tight hearts breathing inside—
> she could never invent them.

Her imaginings are not as realized as the natural cycle in which she has actually taken part and are not of the same value as the unit that she has nurtured, the family, the little time capsule ticking away, which is her real future and as miraculous as any dream that she might conjure up. The final image of the "pocket watch," as a concentrated achievement more potent than the vacancy of daydreaming, is a corrective to fantasy. It is also comically appropriate to Beulah's own intermittent wish to contain her family in a way that does not overwhelm her: if she could shut them up in a pocket watch, they would be a very manageable entity. The efficacy of the image lies in its ambiguity as a figure of Beulah's own desire for control and containment of her responsibilities and as an image of the family held securely in the larger momentum of nature and time.

In middle age, Beulah moves into the sphere of work outside the home, which entails an adjustment of her fantasies as she encounters white racism more directly than when shielded at home. The poem "The Great Palaces of Versailles," in which she does alterations in the back of a dress shop, has the image of "stale Evening of Paris," as if the perfume expresses the disillusionment of her fantasies of European elegance. Yet she remains intrigued and shocked to read of French ladies who "lifting shy layers of silk . . . dropped excrement as daintly / as handkerchieves." One problem for Beulah is the lack of contemporary black role models for women. She both resists and is attracted to cinematic images of white feminine glamor, and she is envious of the way young girls can imitate Lauren Bacall. Unsettling and alluring, these images are a part of Beulah's cultural education. She has to test her fantasies of high civilization against the confusing signals of contemporary mythology that seem to have no place for her, for she is as encaged in the back of the shop as she was at home.

"Pomade" is a key poem in tracing Beulah's self-development. It begins with a typical wifely response to the mess Thomas makes in the house with his fishing tackle but modulates into a memory of a visit to Thomas's sister's home in the South and her perfume-making art is more potent than "stale Evening of Paris." Formerly Beulah had despised Thomas's folk origins, but in his sister, Willemma, she finds, in retrospect, a woman to admire whose life, even more restricted than her own, was lived with spirit and imagination. She could "smell like travel. / But all those years she didn't budge." The hardships of Willemma's life, the primitiveness of the cabin in which she lives, are made evident in the poem, but it is an existence in which the haphazard beauty of the surroundings and feminine skill combine in an authentic poetry:

> That cabin leaned straight away
> to the south, took the very slant of heaven
> through the crabgrass and Queen Anne's Lace to
> the Colored Cemetery down in Wartrace. Barley soup
> yearned toward the bowl's edge, the cornbread
> hot from the oven climbed in glory
> to the very black lip of the cast iron pan . . .

Beulah's memory of her sister-in-law is in part a recall to fundamentals as she thinks about death, but she does not give up her exotic visions: the beebalm that Willemma used puts her "in mind of Turkish minarets." Neither can Beulah resolve the differences between "shoppe," the consumer culture of the North, and "cabin," the rural poverty of the South. Nor can she reconcile the images of segregation or the changing images of the feminine that she has internalized, resisted, or lost. Like that of Dorothea in *Middlemarch,* the influence of her life is "incalculably diffusive,"[31] the larger potential untried.

Artistry in millinery is the nearest that Beulah gets to satisfy her aesthetic instincts. The title "Headdress," referring to the hat she is working on, is a parody on tribal headgear, the strange exoticisms of fashion being equally serious and absurd to an outsider. Beulah, in thrall to the demands of the hat for realization, knows something of the creative buzz. Yet although hat making provides some outlet for her creative energies, the poem that follows, "Sunday Greens," condenses her frustrations. It has the same passionate fury that fills the epigraph to *Canary in Bloom* from Anne Spencer's poem "Lines to a Nasturtium." Beulah is consumed by desire:

> She wants to hear
> wine pouring.
> She wants to taste
> change. She wants
> pride to roar through
> the kitchen . . .
>   she wants
>
> lean

The enjambment spills forward in a sensory frenzy. However, even as she is trapped in the Sunday ritual of a meager dinner in which the ham bone "knocks / in the pot," even at the most furious moment of rebellion, Beulah remembers that her mother was similarly passionate, remembers "those collards / wild-eared, / singing." Whether this memory is consolation or gall to her is left without comment at the end of the poem. But it is a reminder that Beulah does want the American good life and feels her exclusion from it. Future directed in her dreams, she yearns for material pleasures and the gratifications of the senses that these can bring. Her name, after all, signifies the land that shall not be desolate.

The other association of her name with patience is to the fore in the poem "Recovery," in which Thomas convalescing from his heart attack shuffles onto the porch while Beulah remains enigmatically in the parlor. That married life has its distances and silences in adversity is evident in the heavy, claustrophobic atmosphere, the sense of time dragging, of decrepitude. Memory is both a reproach and a resource: "Years ago he had promised to take her to Chicago." Beulah is trapped in her parlor, "secrets like birdsong in the air." This association with her canary, the bird Thomas hates, suggests disaffection, even disloyalty. His slow convalescence involves sacrifice for her. Memory of how he "was lovely then," in the days that were full of promise, keeps her going. The poem is starkly uncompromising about the truths of ageing, the isolating burdens of companionship, the aloneness of marriage, the differences of masculine and feminine perspectives. With Thomas at home all the time, Beulah, losing the porch as a space, retreats into the parlor.

Thomas's death is not presented directly in Beulah's half of the sequence. The poem "Nightmare" seems deliberately non-specific in terms of chronology, as if it could be a premonition of his death or a dream in which the death has reactivated child-hood fears and in which the loss itself is expressed as physical irritation, an "itching." There are elliptical links with the earlier dream poems of the sequence in its registration of emotional disturbance.

In the chronology Dove provides, Thomas's death takes place in 1963, which means that the last three poems in *Canary in Bloom* are of Beulah's experiences as a widow living on for six further years until her death in 1969. "Wingfoot Lake (Independence Day, 1964)" shows Beulah attending a Goodyear Company picnic at her daughters' invitation and remembering the civil rights march on Washington of the previous year. It is a seg-regated picnic, and attending it reminds her of her thirty-sixth birthday, when Thomas had shown her the first swimming pool she had ever seen, with the "swimmers' white arms jutting / into the chevrons of high society." The fact that the persistence of racial segregation is matched in the sixties, by a will for change, sets Beulah thinking about the barriers that she and Thomas faced in their own search for the American dream. Much of the effort that they and others like them put in has been translated into the expansionism of the Goodyear Company, symbolized in the park in which employees are still segregated. The juxtaposition of Beulah's ironic thoughts as the concluding lines with the title of the following poem, "Company," is itself ironic, for Beulah does not feel included in this corporate success story. She is preoccupied with, indeed haunted by, memories of Thomas, debating with him, in a way that she never had while he lived, the questions of what their marriage represented and had achieved. The two poems are very closely linked in their critique of the transitions that Beulah sees their daughters will take part in. For her own part, she acknowledges that "Where she came from / was the past." As she struggles in her emergent politicized awareness, to come to terms with her own sense of thwartedness, she does come to realize and to urge Thomas as she encounters him in dream and memory that "*we were good.*" It is a message she wants to convey to comfort him for the loss of the ordinary things he enjoyed.

Is it possible to argue that the bleakness of the final poem, "The Oriental Ballerina," is mitigated by that realization of their essential goodness? Hardly, in that *Thomas and Beulah* has traced a quest for "life, liberty and the pursuit of happiness," for the American dream in its individualist outlines with all that starkness of expectation. Although Thomas and Beulah have been tied to the fortunes of the Goodyear Company, their fortunes have not been made by it. The color blue traces the suffering that spurs Thomas's outsetting and the cars and swimming pools that mark success or exclusion in their journey. Color marks and divides their passage, the "white foot" of the Good-year Company symbol limiting the blue available. For Beulah as a housewife, mother, and unskilled worker—in the sense of having no profession or training for her artistic talent—her life as she judges it in her final bedridden years, gradually going blind, is unfulfilled. The particular poignancy is that her ambitions have not been narrowly American; she has wanted to travel, to extend her life.

The disparity between Beulah's circumstances, virtually blind and rasping for breath, confined to the narrow round of a sick-room, and "the Orient," where "breath floats like mist / in the fields," is painful. The Orient is the land of the rising sun, and the sun struggles through Beulah's bedroom window, warming her face. This is the moment of her death and the moment of relinquishing the dream: *"There is no China."* The rhyming section of the poem (a rarely used effect in the sequence) grates upon the ear:

> The ballerina has been drilling all night!
> She flaunts her skirts like sails,
> whirling in a disk so bright,

The ballerina has become a mocking figure, the mechanic "drilling" a cruel parody of the searching for beauty and grace that her dance represented. There is no softening of the moment of Beulah's death. The ballerina, the expression of art and the symbol of her hopes of self-development, is finally "impossible."

In "The Oriental Ballerina," Beulah's romantic fantasies are fiercely disallowed as having no connection with the sick-room "stink of camphor." This death is not staged to provide a solace to the reader. The upside-down contrasts are not only geographical but also cultural in the romantic images of "roses drifting" and the "vulgar flowers" of the poor. Beulah's political education has brought her to the point at which she asserts, "*There is no China*," and the narrator of the poem authoritatively endorses the facts of the narrow compass of her opportunities, a life of shabby images, a life dealt a shabby hand of which, at the end, with Beckettian insight, the "head on the pillow," strangely disembodied and divested of the tissue of femininity, states flatly its grim negative.

"Dream Boogie"

"The Oriental Ballerina" is a somber conclusion to the sequence, but in these ordinary lives, there have also been many moments in which life has been grasped and enjoyed. One of the attractions of *Thomas and Beulah* is in the representation of culture as a field of force in which the participants are carried along: the blues, boogie, country folk, and gospel notes that thread the sequence are the potent vehicles of the cultural mythology in which the two protagonists are enfolded. It gives them an idiom in which to dream and desire; sometimes exclusionary, it is nevertheless the ideological hum within which they exist. This is indeed the music of the poem, but it is also realism in that it shows a tension and interplay between the individual consciousness and the social pressures upon that individual. The private dream is the inner space inhabited by the cultural gesture; the social is performed there in that interior theater. The dreamlike quality is in the mingling of the specific evocative detail and the clichés of the American dream.

This is, therefore, Thomas and Beulah's story, but it is also "anybody else's"[32] in the sense that John Ashbery used the phrase to acknowledge how language is culturally ubiquitous and second hand. Dove also recognizes this in the shifts of register between a particularizing fastidiousness and the large overused cultural reflectors in which everyone deals. The affection for the cultural clichés we all inhabit, which invest and enlarge our moods, is apparent in the musical mood structure of the sequence. In musical terms, the swing is between the lightheartedness of a number like "Lightnin's Boogie" in "Courtship" and the histrionic compensations of doleful virtuosity in "Lightnin' Blues." The laid-back inflections of the voice of Lightnin' Hopkins are part of the insouciance of the poem, the quality that it has of "shrugging on down the line,"[33] of moving with a step and a sidle. Like Melvin B. Tolson, Dove asks if the port is worth the cruise, and like Ashbery, she knows that life is process and that we are collectively drenched in the clichés of desire, love, and loss. The seriousness of the *Thomas and Beulah* sequence is lightened by this more caressing, seductive idiom. In her introduction to *Selected Poems,* Dove mentions discovering Langston Hughes's "dazzlingly syncopated" poem "Dream Boogie" as a teenager. It begins:

> Good morning daddy!
> Ain't you heard
> The boogie-woogie rumble
> Of a dream deferred?[34]

It might well have been one of the epigraphs to *Thomas and Beulah,* and I have taken the phrase "a dream deferred" as the subtitle for this chapter not only to register the disappointments of the lives of Thomas and Beulah but also to recognize how Dove positions these lives in the ongoing momentum of the American dream. Dove's sense of cultural syncopation is channeled to more complex purposes, but it is the pulse of the sequence, especially in the *Mandolin* section, where the pleasurable rhythms keep step with the longings and frustrations of the journey. The preoccupation with the ideological import of culture, the glamor, the control mechanisms that create its mythologies, is continued in Dove's next volume, *Grace Notes*. In *Thomas and Beulah*, the syncopations lend life and leniency to a narrative that might otherwise be too austere.

The recovery of African American history is a serious and weighty subject that might have been too portentously rendered were it not for Dove's fluency of expression, which comes at it by so many-angled lights and shadows. The sensitivity of her historical imagination is most active in those glancing intersections between the autobiographical rendering of Thomas and Beulah's own sense of their identities and the omniscient narrator's consciousness of the distance imposed by the passing of time. The acknowledgment of distance signifies respect, but there is also affection: this, after all, is family history as well as the history of the migration of black Americans to the industrial Midwest. Dove's presentation of the "two sides of a story," so that "facts" are susceptible to differing interpretations, situates her own historicist perspective as provisional.

This does, of course, give value to the imagination as an aspect of historical sensibility and fosters a particular kind of self-reflexivity as integral to the structure of the poem. The "assembling vision,"[35] as McDowell has termed the collage-like mode of each individual poem, is a way of making every poem a provisional and tenuous self-referential allusion to the whole rather than an overdetermined plotting of cause and effect. Each one is a fragile construct in which the images steal in, hover, and disperse like tender shades deferential to the "mystery of destiny."[36] It is significant that the one plotted figure, Lem, is acknowledged by Dove as imagined from a lacuna of family history, a cause whose effect was in no way recorded or remembered in any detail in family lore.

There is also, in *Thomas and Beulah,* a sense of ease in human connection, a warmth of feeling in the vernacular touches by which a character comes before us, as "with a quickened difference . . . / strolling up the street," to quote from a Tom Paulin poem, "Anonymous Biography."[37] Paulin develops a distinction in his poem between the painstaking labor of research that recovers and pieces together the details of a life and the capturing of the aura of personality, as if the person was there in actual presence. Biographical recovery is one of Dove's aims, but her characters seem at times to have a kind of insouciance, as if they have just turned up and the talk is sliding around them.

These are conversation poems, then, of a kind that often begin in the middle of a situation to which the reader becomes attuned, as if occasionally privileged to eavesdrop on an ongoing chronicle with gossipy, communal rewards. Yet there is also a Rilkean intensity of being in each individual poem that holds it separate and distinct. Dove herself, in an interview, said of the sequence:

> Each poem is a new field to enter. I wanted each one to be an epiphany, and so I had to enter each poem almost blind. I had the background of all the other poems and all that stuff behind me, but I tried to let it bubble up, rather than trying to just impose it on the page.[38]

It is interesting that Dove uses the image of blindness here that is associated with Beulah, and blindness is an image that Rilke, a poet Dove admires, uses in an epiphanic way. In his poem "Going Blind," the old women feeling her way carefully, with a kind of rapt attention, seems to be "like someone who presently / will have to sing," a figure of creative incipience who will "fly."[39] The realism of Beulah's condition in "The Oriental Ballerina" is perhaps consciously or unconsciously set against this kind of Rilkean lyrical epiphany, but the upwelling, the unique separateness of each individual poem in *Thomas and Beulah* stems from a Rilkean trust in the inwardness and self-sufficiency of each fragment as a new beginning. Beulah has, in any case, symbolized the imagination caged yet seeking flight, and the last poem in which she surrenders vision is only at first anti-Rilkean in its uncompromising resolution. Rilke himself, in one of his last fragments, acknowledged that in the final extremity of sickness or pain, the imagination has to be expelled. "That early wonderment, keep it out of this"[40] is his cry in the face of the obliterations of terminal suffering. Beulah's denial of "China" is similarly a fierce assent to the end of being human, as if to say, keep the imagination out of that degradation, that breaking down of the body, it has no place there.

These are large claims to make about *Thomas and Beulah* in terms of the imaginative range and power to adumbrate a long poem sequence that syncopates the rhythm of culture, adjusts the sensibilities of history, ponders the mysteries of individual destiny, and is open to their mutual constellations. Imbricated in the travails and splendors of the American dream, the sequence affirms the centrality of the dream, for better or worse, for all Americans and critiques its continuing mythology. It is a very American poem, mainstreaming the marginal as many great American writers have done. Writing about it here as an outsider, that fact seems very salient. The American literary canon is now diversifying and extending in remarkable ways, but the effect of this has occasionally been to categorize by subject, to shunt a major work into a siding, in this case labeled African American history. Of course, *Thomas and Beulah* can be read with great inwardness and profit from this documentary perspective, but this would be to ignore not only how Dove has made this *American* history but also the creative power of her achievement. Dove, like Dickens, a voracious childhood reader, has, in the sequence of *Thomas and Beulah*, something of a nineteenth-century novelist's wonder at the mystery of individual identity and belief in the potency of the quotidian detail. This enriches her modernist approach to the crafting of a poem, her postmodernist understanding of the provisionality of such constructions, and her Rilkean and romantic devotion to the fragment. The complexity of her reach is apparent in an approach to form that encompasses the exactitudes of Melvin B. Tolson and Marianne Moore with the speech rhythms of Langston Hughes and John Ashbery. This is not to argue a derivative case but to emphasize that Dove commands that kind of range of idioms. The sequence is rhythmic, self-referential, and intertextual. As Patricia Wallace has noted, Dove's "sensibility . . . is deeply, even passionately literary . . . in conscious relation to (and revision of) other writers"[41] in sophisticated ways. That this complexity always reveals to us the distinctive lives of Thomas and Beulah is the profundity and humanity of Dove's art.

CHAPTER 5

Grace Notes

Stepping off the Tin Roof into Blue

Grace Notes opens with "Summit Beach, 1921." The identification of a racially segregated beach is a historical marker, a bridge with *Thomas and Beulah,* and a point of reference from which to move on. In this collection, Dove considers the enlarged opportunities for herself and her daughter in the America of the 1980s. The volume is thus autobiographical and familial (Summit Lake in Akron was, in fact, where her grandparents first met), but the individual life is registered in relation to the lives of others, and in relation to history, to political conditions, and to ideological aspirations. These concerns, often given mythic expression, explore the common human element in diverse experience: the poet touches the grace notes of famous and unknown lives, past and present. Her elliptical forms are also "notes" in the sense of gleaned scraps, the minimum expression that can honor an identity.

Grace notes in music are embellishments to basic melody, the added notes that might be ornament, sensuous enhancement, or intensity of feeling yet are *adding* something. Dove spoke of her title in an interview with Helen Vendler: "With *Grace Notes* I had several things in mind: every possible meaning of grace, and of notes, and of grace notes, and also a little added riff. In a sense, I am trying to counter the heavy weight of *Thomas and Beulah,* which had such a big scope."[1]

The poem "Canary" is characteristic of the bittersweet tone of the volume. The title recalls Beulah's songbird in the cage, emblematic of her own constriction; it is also the term used by musicians for the singer in a band and, more specifically, evokes Billie Holiday. The images of the singer's grace, despite her damaged life, are held, and just slightly extended like musical phrases, grace notes that display the myth:

> Billie Holiday's burned voice
> had as many shadows as lights,
> a mournful candelabra against a sleek piano,
> the gardenia her signature under that ruined face.

This is like musical notation, but the poet also dryly, sparely notes the "ruined face" and touches upon the injustices and conditions—the reality that burns the voice. This musical sense of phrasing and overall form is a mode that Dove also explored in short fiction: her collection of short stories, *Fifth Sunday,* published in 1985, is bleakly lyrical. Several of the stories are musical in subject and form, but they are also social observation, noting the conflicts of ideologies, the cultural limits that the protagonists struggle to transcend. Similarly, the opening poems of *Grace Notes* are cultural and, furthermore, historical. They are about the environment, the conditions that individuals, in their grace of spirit, have the imagination to amplify and extend.

"Summit Beach, 1921"

Thomas and Beulah concluded with the dissolution of Beulah's dreams. "Summit Beach, 1921," the poem that acts as a prologue to *Grace Notes,* returns to the world of the opening poems of *Mandolin*: the Negro beach, the "mandolin" in the first stanza, and the date, 1921, are a reminder of Thomas's arrival in Akron, his courtship rituals, and the racial prejudice that Dove's grandparents encountered. It laconically documents the racist and gender divisions of that era. *Grace Notes* sets "Summit Beach, 1921" as a historical marker to gauge the possibilities for young black American women sixty years on from the conditions of the 1920s.

As such, it affirms a feminist perspective as the starting point for the volume: the black adolescent girl (similar to Beulah) on Summit Beach is alive to the same rhythms and desires as the men, but she has to behave differently, to exercise a wary self-restraint. Her scarred knee, which had "itched" in the plaster cast, and her "shawl moored by a fake cameo" are emblematic of her static condition, her constricted life choices. Her adventure of the spirit lies in the hazard of waiting and responding to "the right man." The small tokens of her regard that she allows the boys are as studied as a medieval chivalric code, "neat as a dropped hankie." There is a poignant contrast between her adolescent guarded constraint and the confidence of her childhood, when, Icarus-like, "she climbed Papa's shed and stepped off / the tin roof into blue."[2] The sensory freedom of childhood has been replaced by wariness; she fell off the roof and cut her knee. Schooled, too, by parental advice, the girl now refuses "to cut the wing." However, as Bonnie Costello has noted, the dreams of love with which she is preoccupied are like "invisible wings," compensating for the way she has been "betrayed by the reality around her,"[3] the racially segregated beach. The cultural terms of segregation frame the volume as well as the poem: the "invisible wings" of the spirit, the "skittering" music of sensory delight are the grace notes picked out in a "mean" context.

Refusing Contemplation

The autobiographical poems that follow have a deliberately rough texture, like an album of snapshots that has not been sorted, a haphazard documenting of family life. The wary step-by-step positioning of the series about the poet's father, "My Father's Telescope," in *Museum* has been replaced in *Grace Notes* by a more communal mode. It is significant that Dove roots her poetic vocation not in Wordsworthian separations and exaltations but in the ordinary sibling rivalries and intergenerational impatiences that both cramp and energize people. The poems of childhood range from the rooted "Fifth Grade Autobiography" to the mean realism of "The Buckeye," in which the brute physicality of children kicking buckeye fruit signals at once their aggressions and their potentiality, lying in wait to ambush the future.

Two adjacent poems, "Crab-Boil," subtitled "*(Ft. Myers, 1962)*," and "Hully Gully," link back to "Summit Beach, 1921." Sixty years has hardly altered racial segregation on a (Florida) beach in the South. What has changed is the attitude of the young black girl, Dove herself, who is not static like her predecessor, but full of questions, boiling with anger. The crabs in the bucket are a multiple image: to the aunt, who has internalized the negative stereotypes of southern ideology, "a bunch of niggers" contained by their own ineptitude; to the girl, an expression of her own distress and anger at the inequalities of segregation and of her aunt's acceptance of racist stereotypes. But for the girl, the crabs are also a focus for feelings of revenge, and of exorcism of those feelings. Cooked, the crabs are "merely exotic, / a blushing meat." The image retains the desire to reverse the stereotyping, the brutality of "meat," now white meat rather than nigger meat, but the "boil" of feeling is redirected, although hardly contained. Aunt Helen is excused: "After all, she *has* / grown old in the South." But her niece, raised in the North, is more belligerent: "If / we're kicked out now, I'm ready." This child does not wait and dream but makes choices about what to believe. The power of the poem, as a microcosm of culturally induced racial tension, lies in its determination not to smooth over the jagged mix of feelings: the shamefulness of "angry pink beseeching" and the dehumanizing of "they don't feel a thing." The crabs are too close for comfort; they scratch at the scab of old scars, and their carapaces are like those of human exclusion zones.

The racial and family discomforts of "Crab-Boil" are suspended in "Hully Gully" (the title comes from a popular song and dance tune), in which the generations are lulled in the hum of summer: the daughters are "daydreaming" in the present participle endlessness of youth while, already consigned to the past tense, their grandmothers "rocked," their fathers "worked," and "wives straightened oval photographs / above the exhausted chenille / in bedrooms upstairs everywhere." The poem condenses pulse and ebb, as if a contraction of Whitmanesque expansiveness, as if the dynamic of Whitman's famous life-cycle poems, "Out of the Cradle Endlessly Rocking" and "As I Ebb'd with the Ocean of Life,"[4] had been distilled into a fantasia of summer in which the cultural and natural rhythms of the generations are evoked with an exactness of detail: the girls leaning "their elbows / into the shells of lemons" particularize the musical hum of culture and nature. The generations are caught up in a collective dream, a theater in which the "personae of summer"[5] play their parts.

Childhood and the family, as dream bank, arena of sibling rivalry, and narrative resource in providing unsuitable uncles retailing mythical sexploits ("Uncle Millet"), are not, however, automatically given uncritical enhancement. The final poem of the first section is "Poem in Which I Refuse Contemplation." Harassed international poet, mother, wife, and menstruating woman, she arrives in Germany, where her mother's letter is waiting for her. It is a pressure and a recall to a known "language"; the misspellings and assumptions irritate:

> *The roses are flurishing.*

> Haven't I always hated gardening?

Yet it is also a reassurance and a pull back to origins: the menstrual "cramp and leak" of the exhausted body is an imperfect version of the flow of memory, the return of water to "where it was" (a quotation from the Toni Morrison epigraph to section 1 of *Grace Notes*).

Mythic Particularities

The epigraphs to section 2 of *Grace Notes* suggest the self as a secret "garden," a "forbidden fruit," as if to tap into the psyche is to recover an Edenic source. The poems that follow are concerned with the thresholds of the mind, with the strange paradoxes of sentience resurgent. The first poem, "Mississippi," implodes with a sensual authority, declaring itself as the code of primal narrative and, within a few lines, as potent individual memory. The poem is very short, concentrating biblical, cultural, and sensual beginnings into mythic intensity:

> In the beginning was the dark
> moan and creak, a sidewheel
> moving through.

This is both a new sexual encounter and a Mississippi river boat. Erotic intensity is expressed as nature in the early paradisal time penetrated by culture, "Thicker / then, scent of lilac, / scent of thyme." The seduction of the lover and the territorially unknown are infused each with the other:

> We were falling down
> river, carnal
> slippage and shadow melt.
> We were standing on the deck
> of the New World, before maps:

The fall into sexuality is both "carnal / slippage" and "the deck / of the New World," paradoxically compressing biblical expulsion and start up, as well as extremes of scale from individual to national destiny. Sexuality here is the engine of being and the metaphor of American discovery.

Mythic and manifest destiny, however, is subject to geography and climate. The throb of energy that delights in and explores the sexual and geographical garden finds itself, in Mississippi, dissipated in the very motion of progress: the hissing steam of the river boat evaporates into the humid atmosphere, a symbol of the enervated "spirit hissing away." In another way, too, this Eden has the "shadow" of what comes after: the postlapsarian world of exploration and "maps" is also the heart of darkness, the world of slavery in which "the dark / moan and creak" has a different meaning. Historically, the river has been a race memory, as Langston Hughes invokes in "The Negro Speaks of Rivers,"[6] yet also a passage, a journey toward freedom or servitude, a cultural self-discovery for good or evil. Dove's poem makes much of its indeterminacy of scale, its mediation between historical resonance and an autobiographical inflection that is teasingly private. "Mississippi" condenses epic grandeur and erotic intimacy in the rise and fall rhythm from the opening phrase, "In the beginning," to the closing post-coitus leak of spirit. Dove's artistic success in "Mississippi" in creating a succinct mythic form of particularized sensory immediacy that also carries a charge of memory, cultural and personal, is a blueprint for *Mother Love* (1995), the volume in which these powers are most fully extended.

If "Mississippi" expresses the sensory power of nature, the poem "Ozone" asks if humans are destroying nature. It sets up cosmic questionings intertextually in relation to the epigraph from Rilke's "Second Elegy":

> *. . . Does the cosmic*
> *space we dissolve into taste of us, then?*

Dove has the Rilkean desire to *taste* the cosmic, both to lose the self "in the wreckage of the moment" and to feel that the sensory is the sign of our participation in the cosmic current, as if we are not lost but somehow dispersed out there. However, the Rilkean epigraph has its twenty-first-century ironies. The "dome of heaven" has been pierced by the space rocket but also perforated by the "aerosol can" of modern convenience culture. The "taste of us" is not sensory delight but the trash that we leave in our wake, the damage done to the ozone layer so that it no longer protects us from harmful radiation. Dove's poem is permeated with images of wiring, threading, and puncturing, the diligent and egotistical human efforts to arrange and control nature, which are also damaging and "constantly / unraveling": our imaginations are more comfortable with ideas of control and proximity than with the unknowable.

Rilke's "Second Elegy" is the most passionate of the *Duino Elegies,* combining *terribilità* and a desire to give human physicality a more than temporal existence. Lamenting that each breath is loss—"oh, we breathe ourselves out and away"—yet aware that lovers' embraces "almost promise eternity,"[7] the poem expresses the desire to transcend mortality but also celebrates the intimate space of humanity. Dove's questioning is as urgent, but more exasperated, forsaking elevation:

> *Where does it go then,*
> *atmosphere suckered up*
> *an invisible flue?*
> *How can we know where it goes?*

Rilke positions love center-stage and asks, in contemplating "Attic stelae," if it does not seem that love is divinely conferred, a supernatural trace element:

> Were not love and farewell
> so lightly laid upon shoulders, they seemed to be made
> of other stuff than us?

Dove's image for human proximity is not that of lovers but neighbors, and the image is discomforting rather than dignified, not "Attic stelae," but teeth crowded together in a mouth, an involuntary contiguity and dependence. Civilization is not so much the self-mastery that Rilke admired in the Greek sculptors as the inability to escape from the wreckage we have created, whether personal or collective. Clichés such as *"to pull the plug"* rattle emptily against the sense of lost Rilkean sublimities, but there is the same questioning of existence and of connection between the intimate and the supra-human scale, which evaporates at the moment of apprehension.

Such cosmic intensities cannot be sustained however, and the concluding poems of the section return to a more personal note. In "Your Death," the day of the demise of the poet's father-in-law is also the day her pregnancy is confirmed. The conflicting tug of emotion, the sense of the imperative competing presences of the dead and the unborn, the family-cycle asserting itself relentlessly, is also evident in the related poem "The Wake." The poet, pregnant daughter-in-law, lies in bed, almost as if in a winding sheet, suspended between the two states, absenting herself from the weeping relatives below, withdrawing into the single-minded concentration of pregnancy.

The Dream of Maternity

The poems of the third section of *Grace Notes* are about the pleasures and pains of motherhood. "Pastoral," a poem about breast-feeding, expresses the enthrallments of a new-born baby, "Like an otter, but warm," but it is tender *and* precise: "I watched diminished / by those amazing gulps." The distinction, "I liked afterwards best," is a sensory revel as much as a report, yet it is an everyday satisfaction, colloquially expressed, that gives license to the pastoralism. The freedom of desire in this poem is deliberately compromised or complicated in the poems that follow. Culture necessarily imposes itself upon nature; the dreamlike state of maternity gives way to the mythic narratives with which parents console and condition children.

In this respect, the poem "Horse and Tree" is conceived in the antithesis and connection between the two elements of the title. The tree represents the freedom of nature—the sap rising, all the conventional attributes of trees. It is also what infants are encouraged in kindergarten to imagine themselves to be and therefore functions as a cultural metaphor. In the poem, the idea of riding the tree, the imaginative extension of movement, is "why horses were invented, and saddles / tooled with singular stars." These "invented" horses are "carousel" horses: the image has become that of life as a mechanical fairground, which small children fear to get onto because "it insists that life is round." Culture grinds and tools the imagery, coarsens and stamps us, yet parents, caught themselves in the process of culture and nature, find in their children heart-aching renewal and wonder:

> children
> might fear a carousel at first for the way
> it insists that life is round. No,
>
> we reply, there is music and then it stops;
> the beautiful is always rising and falling.
> We call and the children sing back *one more time*.
> In the tree the luminous sap ascends.

This expresses how the entry into culture is a diminishment, a carousel onto which children step with fearful hesitancy, and yet also the source of confidence and pleasure, a conformity and a starting out, "*one more time*." Dove's sensibility is not so much a Wordsworthian premonition of "shades of the prison-house"[8] closing around the child. Rather, it has an intertextual affinity to Rilke's "Merry-Go-Round,"[9] a poem in which the rapid motion expresses both the blissfully ecstatic setting out of the children and the more adult understanding of transience, the terrifyingly short time "until it's ended." In Rilke's poem, the children are passengers, "blindly following fun," whereas Dove's stance is less distanced and more involved: "We call and the children sing back." It is, as if in reply to Rilke, she acknowledges how the merry-go-round asserts its claims as an ominous image both of the constraints of culture and of the brief passage of our lives. Yet for her, the rise and fall motion is also expressive of the natural and familial cycle in which as sensory beings we are a vital part, and, in caring for our children, in sharing aesthetic delight and loss—"the beautiful is always rising and falling"—we have something that is life giving, a natural joy.

There is scant nature in "The Breathing, the Endless News," a poem about childhood acculturation. Culture gives us mythic identity. It is a god before which we abase ourselves. The paradox is that a god becomes a mythic "receptacle," the dumping ground for all the cultural trash we generate; we fill the gods "with the myth of ourselves," yet we also have the belief that children are "the trailings of gods." So we fill them, too, with the myth of ourselves, which they play out upon their dolls. The dolls are not capable of growth, "no blossoming there," but the children, more ominously, know just what to do. They shoot the dolls; they have been ideologically imprinted:

> With every execution
> doll and god grow stronger.

With each sign that they have absorbed the violence of culture, the children demonstrate their subservience to the gods that culture worships. This is a chilling little poem, an antidote to the lyricism of "Pastoral." It moves with a measured causal inevitability, a macabre comedy of fulfillment, pitched between awe and satire. The laconic *enjambments* suspend and then spill the beans unexpectedly, pitching high when you expect cynicism:

> Children know this: they are
> the trailings of gods.

However, such declarative language is incongruously juxta-posed with the doll images "slumped over," "out for the count": the mythic is not just "elk horn, / cloven hoof" but the domain of the demotic. The careful crafting of this poem in its compact-ing of the contemporary and the antique prefigures the meta-phorical and critical intelligence of *Mother Love*.

The poem "After Reading *Mickey in the Night Kitchen* for the Third Time before Bed" (the extended title mimetically echoing an experience parents will recognize) has achieved some fame through Dove's public readings of it, moving subjects on to the poetic agenda that might seem programmatically femi-nist. As often with Dove, the terms of the agenda are changed. The opening seems didactic, as if this is a poem about politically correct liberal frankness. It *deals* with the worthy feminist topic of a mother teaching her daughter about genitalia and menstru-ation, but it has a nice punning conclusion that conflates inter-nal anatomy, racial composition, and well-being.

Wit is notably Dove's way of approaching racial issues in *Grace Notes*. The title of the poem "Genetic Expedition" sig-nals the analytical coolness of this reading of Elizabeth Bishop's autobiographical poem "In the Waiting Room"[10] from an Afri-can American adult woman's perspective. Bishop's poem enacts a child's crisis of identity at the idea of being female. Appalled by the pictures of "black naked women" in the *National Geo-graphic* ("Their breasts were horrifying"), the young Elizabeth recoils from adulthood, from becoming like her aunt, from becoming "one of *them*," the awful community of the adult fem-inine whose exotic alien status is signaled by the photographs in the journal that, as Dove ironically notes in her poem, "my father forbade us to read." The opening lines on maternity and racial characteristics in "Genetic Expedition" are wryly analytical, a turning of the tables in relation to Bishop's poem:

> Each evening I see my breasts
> slacker, black-tipped
> like the heavy plugs on hot water bottles;
> each day resembling more the spiked fruits
> dangling from natives in the *National Geographic*

Maternity is both domestic and exotic, and neither nudity nor blackness are such a cultural shock as in 1918, the date of the events in the Bishop poem. Dove, married to a German writer, with a mixed-race daughter at whom people stare, is able to renegotiate cultural stereotypes. Living among them and subject to them, she redeploys them, just as she refigures Bishop's "In the Waiting Room." It is characteristic that Dove finds common ground with the images of the poem, in this way, fashioning a world in which her daughter can flourish and using language, in the words of the epigraph of this section, as "a talisman to hold against the world."

The poetry of this third section is experimental, at times revisiting the confessional mode. As did Robert Lowell, Dove combines the expression of family and parenthood with a critical take on American culture. However, in the 1980s, there are international opportunities: this is a life of "jet-lag and laundry," a world away from "Summit Beach, 1921." This is an America of multicultural diversity, but it is also ideologically homogenous, with media-driven myths of identity in whose capacious maws our children are easily swallowed up. Yet in spite of the dangers of blandness and conformity, "the beautiful is always rising and falling": the rhythm of the natural cycle is, at times, in harmony with the carousel of culture.

Section 3, for all the focus on maternity and the joys and cares of parenthood, concludes with a poem about personal space. In "Backyard, 6 A.M.," the poet, returning home after an overnight flight, is burdened by the sense of duty and constraint. Yet the "wings" of the spirit "quickening," the sense of artistic vocation making its way against hindrance, is the subject of the next section.

Poetic Dedication

Section 4 is politically tougher, more resolute than the previous sections: it records a renewed dedication to the art of poetry. The first poem, "Dedication," subtitled "*after Czeslaw Milosz*," is a tribute to "quiet," a turning back to essentials, to "hill" and "brook." In American terms, this echoes Robert Frost's poem "Directive,"[11] in which the poet, casting a spell upon the reader, "only has at heart your getting lost." Dove wistfully

> wanted only to know
>
> what I had missed, early on—
> that ironic half-salute of the truly lost.

But Dove is not about to become a nature poet; she has cultural battles to fight, as "Ars Poetica," the poem that follows, makes clear. The poem anecdotally recalls the self-importance of male writers, one trying to impose himself upon the colossal scale of the Wyoming landscape and another avoiding learning to cook in the pursuit of his genius. From such gender irritants, the poem develops, as the poet recognized, into a "self-conscious declaration of literary philosophy."[12] The art of poetry, for Dove, involves rising above the masculine ego and acknowledging the resistance of American landscape to the individual mind: "the long dull stare of Wyoming" can outface a "terribly important essayist," but the solution is to be both "small" and powerfully in flight:

> What I want is this poem to be small,
> a ghost town
> on the larger map of wills.
> Then you can pencil me in as a hawk:
> a traveling x-marks-the-spot.

This is a beautifully poised expression of the imagination as aerial, free, and precise and, as Therese Steffen has commented, the "x" "has historically significant connotations: "the signature of someone who cannot write," particularly a "slave's anonymous hand." It is "an identification with the nameless and forgotten."[13] "Ars Poetica," which seems at first a sardonic undermining of "Dedication," becomes a re-visioning of its concerns.

It is not always possible to maintain a lofty superiority to cultural dreck. The poem "Arrow" might seem to recall Sylvia Plath's "Ariel," in which the feminine poet-persona refashions herself in the incandescent heat of creativity, unpeeling masculine "dead hands, dead stringencies,"[14] but Dove's poem remains resolutely terrestrial. It is a comic vignette of the racist and sexist condescension of a literary critic and the responses of the black women in the audience of his lecture. Debating "their different ways of coping," the poem remains unresolved about strategy but it makes clear that "pencil me in as a hawk" is not always a possible or even desirable option. Poetry cannot absent itself from the attritions of professional life. These are, after all, the wounds, the scarring of the spirit for which verbal toughness is a survival mechanism.

The section as a whole is concerned with how we talk about experience and whether what we think of as being experience is a drain or an inspiration to poetry. The poem "And Counting" ironically savors the pleasures of having been awarded a month's residency at the Villa Serbelloni Study and Conference Center in Bellagio, Italy. The place is so beautiful and the daily pleasures so enchanting that poetic composition gets lost. The colloquial wise-cracking idiom comically rehearses the sense of unfitness for the privilege: "Well of course I'm not worth it but neither is / the Taj Mahal for that matter so who's counting?" And of course, in spite of being "put . . . under" by "pasta," the poem does get written.

The final poem of section 4, "In a Neutral City," is pessimistic in declaring that conversation is what will remain in old age as a poor compensation for the sensory experiences that we have lost, but it also suggests that memory might filter in before the "worms":

> over lunch we will search for a topic
> only to remember a hill, a path hushed
> in the waxen shade of magnolias.

Memory as life in death or death in life is evoked here in "the waxen shade of magnolias," which is both vivifying recall in the face of coming extinction and premonitory of the "waxen shade" of death.

"In a Neutral City" delves into uncomfortable subjects such as decay and loss of powers, and in this respect, it is the obverse of the previous poem, "Medusa," which is a condensed prefiguration of artistic power. Medusa (the name means "ruler" or "queen") is from the ocean; she is also the gorgon whose stare can turn to stone. From this paradox of liquid depth and petrified form, creative power emanates. Helen Vendler has interpreted this poem in terms of blackness, and I would agree that "the dark delight of being strange," the quotation from Claude McKay that Dove has chosen as the epigraph to section 4, suggests, as Vendler says, "blackness . . . as the first skin of consciousness."[15] It may well be the case that the "dark delight" is racially inflected. But it seems to me that "Medusa" is primarily about the assumption of poetic power, gendered, declarative, and sensuously originary:

> I've got to go
> down where my eye
> can't reach
> hairy star
> who forgets to shiver
> forgets the cool suck
> inside

The poem focuses the myth very attentively, and in doing so, it metaphorizes and resolves the debate in the preceding poems about the conscious and the less conscious origins of poetry. The "hairy star" of the eye, the organ of critical scrutiny, "can't reach" or "forgets" the "cool suck" of sensory origins," an image at once vaginal and oceanic. The sea is amniotic fluid and (as in the Toni Morrison epigraph to section 1) the flow of memory and life back to their source, the eternal cyclic return to the maternal embrace of death. "Medusa" is a regal acknowledgment of sexuality, of the dark underside of the psyche, the mysteriousness and penetration of its reach (Medusa's ghost went to Hades' kingdom in the underworld and frightened the shades of the dead).

All this is source. There is also the end product. One way to exercise power, to be queen, as Sylvia Plath prophesied in the final poetry that mythicized her, is in the posthumous life of the poems, released from the "woman" into the hard, classical stasis of art. Medusa, killed by Perseus, had a posthumous life in art. Athena, goddess of wisdom, set Medusa's head in the center of her breastplate; the blood from the neck of Medusa's decapitated corpse gave birth to Pegasus, the winged horse of poetry. Dove mines the myth as poetic power rather than as female stereotype. Whereas Hélène Cixous used the Medusa myth for feminist consciousness-raising,[16] Dove focuses precisely on origin and result. The triumphant raising of Medusa's head by Perseus is an image of poetic canonization. This will be both stellification and petrification:

> Someday long
> off someone will
> see me
> fling me up
> until I hook
> into sky
>
> drop his memory
>
> My hair
> dry water

The idea of the poem as "dry water," a kind of petrified relic of the "shiver" of its inception, is a curious paradox. Or is the poem now, as Vendler suggests, an "astral cold, something like a halo of icicles"?[17] Whichever, the effect is of the separative, metamorphic, transformative power of art that leaves behind the personal. The ambiguity of "drop his memory" refers to rising above what Perseus has done but also, in a more directly gendered sense, to abandoning patriarchy, and in formalist terms the "hook / into sky" is the immortality of the canonized work of art transcending the pain of life. The condensed sensory delight and pain, the hard / soft, dry / wet, interior pleasure / exterior rough conjunctions are both abrasive and lyric. It has the shiver and chill of a Billie Holiday song: she found, from within, the grace notes of a damaged life, thrown up as she was by the public into stardom. Understatement and compression give the poem cryptic resonance, a mesmerizing aura distilled in "dry water," the oxymoronic conclusion.

Things Elsewhere

The epigraph from Cavafy to section 5 of *Grace Notes* begins "Don't hope for things elsewhere / Now that you've wasted your life here." It warns that the individual life, in its "small corner," is a part of the whole; the damage that is individually and locally inflicted destroys "everywhere." The opening poems of this final section of the volume change gear: they move away from the privilege of autobiography and personal poetic dedication, from Rilkean questionings of the ozone layer. The focus moves to the blighted conditions of black communities in American culture: maternity, family life, and prospects. What is "wasted" in this not so "small corner" of American life? What local damage infects "everywhere"?

Dove's poetic technique in this section is to express what might conventionally be regarded as deprivation in a narrative fragment that reconceives the value of the individual life as historically representative. The first poem, "Saints," is structured on the analogy of Catholic rituals and the birth pangs of a black mother of many children. The plurality of the title suggests that sainthood can be found in different cultures in different ways. The mother's birthing is like counting the beads on a rosary: frequency become ritualistic yet casually domestic, and she is herself religious, not just metaphorical object but subject. This fat woman, who "stinks in warm weather," attends church. "She'll pin on a hat, groan into a pew" with a devotional fervor visionary in capacity. She believes in the freedom promised in the refrain of the gospel hymn "Michael, Row the Boat Ashore," in the crossing of the River Jordan to liberty, in the archangel, Michael's militant championing of good.

The third and final verse of the poem expands into a community of souls, as if all her children are the congregation in the church, but with a difference. The image transmutes into one of martyrdom, dismemberment, and lynching. They are not in the pews but strung up incongruously like devotional images:

> They are like the tin replicas of eyes and limbs
> hung up in small churches,
> meticulous
> cages, medallions
> swinging in the dazed air.

The martyred bodies, an involuntary sainthood, become a visual image ironically like the rather grisly votive offerings made to traditional saints asking for cures and intercessions. At birth, each one was a "freedom," a relief for the mother from pregnancy and a new life constitutionally endowed. Now, the "meticulous cages" of their trussed bodies are neatly emblematic of their cultural representativeness as victims of racism, "hung" like the "trophies"[18] in Keats's "Ode on Melancholy," and like the speaker of Keats's poem, *they themselves* are the trophies. They are not represented by objects, they are the objects.

The power of the poem resides in the way the opening witty analogy between medieval and modern sainthood shifts its ground from the theme of feminine endurance and issues of religion or religiosity to the political. From whose perspective are the offspring envisaged as "like . . . medallions," classical trophies, or as religious votive offerings, the ritualized mode of representation transmuting into the political reality? The perspective is one distinctly separate from the devotional imaginings and rituals of the black woman; the speaker of the poem exasperatedly questions her religious habits and her superstitious credulity. Yet the word "dazed" used in the last line is appropriate to all who try to imagine those who were victims of brutalities "perishing under the rafters!" The image is both deliberate, "they are like," and stupefyingly remote, not as unlike the position of the woman, the religious believer, as the more skeptical mind might expect. The working through of the poem induces discomfort. There are the things that we are easily separate from and might regard ourselves as superior to, then there are the things that we are so far from apprehending that they can only be mysterious and remote. Dove defamiliarizes our ideological assumptions, to reposition us more precisely at a greater distance. Saints, however ideologically packaged or trussed, have been, to pick up Cavafy's phrase again, "destroyed" in every small corner of the world in the name of a particular ideology. This familiar idea is paradoxically remote in that the transformation into martyrdom is incomprehensible to those who have not suffered it. Those who have undergone it are separate now.

The poem "The Gorge," in a blues idiom, is also "poor man's history," to quote from its concluding line. Little Joe tried to escape from his bullying father but sat down by the railroad track to cry and had his toe cut off by the train. The poem, in its comically doleful despairing rhythm, captures of small town claustrophobia:

> That's

> Why they carried little Joe
> Home and why his toe
> Ain't never coming back. Oh

The bathos of being reduced from the grand gesture of leaving town is accentuated by the fact that even the stream in the gorge leaves town; it dries up in the summer. "Little Cuyahoga's done up left town" is expressed in stereotypical folk idiom as a swaggering gesture, but Little Joe can not even put a toe out of town. The laconic cruelty of the small-town anecdote is neatly captured in the deployment of clichéd phrases that mimic the fatalism of the episode. Dove, in talking about the poem, said, "Myth begins in anecdote,"[19] and the poem cycles anecdote and nature, processing them into the first stage of becoming myth: "This gorge leaves a trail / Of anecdotes." The detritus left on the bed of the once swollen river is "April's arthritic magnitude," an ironic allusion perhaps to "April is the cruelest month," the opening passage of T. S. Eliot's mythic *The Waste Land*, "breeding / Lilacs"[20] out of the corpse-ridden postwar landscape.

Freedom and denial of freedom is the accent of the first four poems of section 5, most poignantly, yet with a critique of that poignancy, in "Canary" about Billie Holiday. The poem is dedicated to the poet Michael Harper. Dove said that his use of

"Blues and Jazz idioms" always "nourished"[21] her writing. There is a musical modulation in the poem: the first stanza (quoted in the opening of this chapter) is an elegaic evocation of her "burned voice" as expressive of her damaged life; the second stanza, in parentheses, swings into the instrumental interplay of the jazz idiom to express the high of jazz and addiction: "(Now you're cooking, drummer to bass, / magic spoon, magic needle. . . .)" The third stanza laconically notes that the effect of mythicizing her life is also to "sharpen" the myth of love. The final line, set off from the rest of the poem, "If you can't be free, be a mystery," is a comment on the way in which Holiday got the myth rather than freedom, but it is also a tribute, as Dove said in an interview, to the way the singer "prevailed against such debilitating odds": "That insistence on style—not 'style' in the sense of putting on a show, but how you carry yourself through the world—is what earned her the title Lady Day."[22]

The experimentation with voice in these poems plays the colloquial against the lyrical and the clichéd against the individual subjectivity in ways that highlight the constraints of these lives. Myths of sainthood, family life, and masculine liberty and feminine mystery have a "signature" language that is tested against the dereliction of human existence.

In contrast, the final poems of section 5 open out geographically and culturally. In some of the poems, this is a liberating perspective. Orchestrating a range of locations from Paris to Israel, Dove turns to the longer sweep of culture and history, and the mythic now seems a realm, enhancing and enchanting, an aura to be assumed. "The Island Women of Paris" is a poem of comic bravura; the exoticism, the *difference* of black women in Paris is celebrated in a series of metaphors that express their regality of motion and bearing. They "skim from curb to curb like regatta," "each a country to herself." The emphasis is on imaginative freedom rather than constraint:

> The island women move through Paris
> as if they had just finished inventing
> their destinations.

Dove said of this poem that in Paris she learned that "gazing at another person was not construed as being impolite. . . . It taught me something about being able to bear up under scrutiny with grace."[23]

The musical dimension of this volume is enriched by the poem "Obbligato." It has as an epigraph a declaration of love in a letter from the romantic composer Berlioz to Madame F. that begins "*Consider that I have loved you for forty-nine years*" and then goes on to affirm his continuing love. The term "obbligato" in music, when attached to the part of an instrument on a score, means that it is essential to the effect and must not be omitted. From what is known of Berlioz biographically, it would seem that Madame F. was a childhood sweetheart on whose "pink shoes" he was fixated, but she was later superseded by other passions. Berlioz married twice, but when he and Madame F. were both widowed, he sought her out again with declarations such as the one in the epigraph. The prime obligation for Berlioz was the obligation to love, an imperative that overrides questions about the accuracy of this particular declaration to Madame F. in terms of constancy (Irish Shakespearian actress Harriet Smithson was another of his grand passions). It is the passionate commitment to love itself as an ideal that is the obbligato, the element essential to the effect. Similarly, in terms of poetic form, without the idea of romantic passion and the passion for music, the parts of "Obbligato" seem like sketchy notes, unfinished jottings in the sense that Dove described as part of her meaning for the volume title. They do not compose: they neither make any kind of narrative connection nor become an ensemble:

> The murmured solicitudes, the gloves.
>
> He could debate the existence of God, describe
> the vexed look on the face of the timpanist
> who had never heard of felt-tips. Or the trumpets
> failing their entrance in *Iphegenie*—

The poem plays on the notion of obligation, registering other kinds of obligation in Berlioz's life, beginning with the tedium and nervousness of depending on patrons: awkward in polite company, he spills the tea, yet he is a man who, as music critic of the *Journal des Débats*, "could debate the existence of God" and had the most acute ear for the technicalities of performance. In his *Treatise on the Orchestra* of 1843, Berlioz discusses the respective quality of drumsticks covered in different materials, including "felt-tips." His admiration for Gluck would have made him appreciative of Gluck's intentions in *Iphigenie in Tauride* in using the orchestra to express Orestes' inner agitation while the character on stage remains outwardly calm. The orchestra at the first rehearsal of the opera failed to understand and faltered, "the trumpets / failing their entrance." All these allusions or fragments of information that make up the poem chart the *idées fixes* of Berlioz's romantic passions in music and love, across which there is the drift of polite trivialities, the other kinds of obligations of his life. The final line, "Invisible command, the enemy everywhere," affirms that in his beleaguered life, his love and his music are his inner power; love both afflicts and energizes.

Berlioz wrote, "*I know the world and have no illusions,*" yet, paradoxically, this obligation to deal in worldly considerations has not quenched "*illusions,*" the passionate belief in love that is the obbligato to the score of his life. Berlioz's life is that of a self-declared romantic, obsessively dedicated to technical innovation, beset by ordinary irritations and financial difficulties, swayed and centered by passion—in fact, a mythic life, exemplary of the romantic artist. The modernist form of the poem, which works by accumulated allusions, creates a surface dryness, but the irony is not at Berlioz's expense. Unlike Prufrock, Eliot's debilitated postromantic protagonist, the obligations of Berlioz's life were those of romantic destiny. Dove has always been interested in capturing the imaginative capacity of an individual's life (which includes, as in Berlioz's case, the capacity to imagine its own romantic trajectory) within the concise form of poetry. The life might be ordinary or famous, but she has a particular tenderness for the fallibilities and manias of the life of a musical creative genius (as also, for example, in her early comic poem, "Robert Schumann, or: Musical Genius Begins with Affliction"). The selectivity of detail in both the Schumann and the Berlioz poems is a reminder of the small basis on which the mythology of the lives of the famous is created. It is also a response to the driven nature of genius, that which gives form to the sprawling inconsistencies of their quotidian existence.

The mundane detail of people's lives, the episode that seems representative, is an aspect of Dove's respect for the narrative moment but also an acute sense of how arbitrary the process of narrative shaping is, how so few elements create a "story." The elements of story can sometimes seem "an awkward loveliness," a phrase from the poem "Lint," which follows "Obbligato." "Lint" is ambivalent about the "noise," the "lint" with which we fill up existence or, for that matter, poems. Although Dove's poetry so often has the narrative fragment as a formal element, this is in tension with the attraction of distanced economy:

> How good to revolve
>
> on the edge of a system—
> small, unimaginable, cold.

The six two-line stanzas of "Lint" are expressive of the desire to be "small," reminiscent of "Ars Poetica."

The last three poems of the volume, set in Israel, return to a more politicized engagement, to the dictates of militant ideologies and their effects on individual lives. There is also a return, in structure, to the power of narrative to set off, to make salient. Discrete narrative elements acquire meaning by conjunction. The poem "The Royal Workshops" reflects on the artifacts that are the residue of a political system and, in particular, the dependence of art upon slavery in many cultures. In the poem "Lint," the "Blue is all around," but for art, the creation of blue is the product of slave labor, the work of the "Jew, the wretched dyer." The snail slime that fixes the dyeing process becomes a commodity to trade with and fight over. The poem is set out in numbered verse paragraphs like those in the Bible. Beginning with the conjunction of the natural habitat of the snails and the two kettles of blue and red, which would be mixed to make royal purple, symbolically expressive of the art and blood that goes into its creation, the poem concludes with a resumé of the cultural mix that, ostensibly blended in the service of God, becomes an instrument of aggression:

6
Slave's work, to wring and dry and drape;
man's work to adorn the unspeakable.
Evening lavishes shade on a cold battlefield
as God retreats

before a fanfare of trumpets and heliotrope.

The conjunction of salt and slime as economic advantage is amusingly rendered in the dialogue between God and the Jewish dyer, Zebulun, who feels that it was unfair that he was only given a snail while his brother was given countries. God, of course, knows that the demand for royal purple dye will be insatiable.

This kind of artful reshaping of biblical narrative is particularly alluring in "On the Road to Damascus." It has as an epigraph Acts 22:6–7 of the New Testament, in which Paul himself retells the story of his conversion that has already been given in Acts 9. The poem plays on the process by which a version of a story in circulation becomes the definitive version. So the poem begins with Paul's irritated voice—"They say I was struck down by the voice of an angel"—as he attempts to put forward his own version. This is more a recall of the physical shock of the event rather than the religious interpretation, the version honed by his attendants:

My first recollection was of Unbroken Blue—
but two of the guards have already sworn by
the tip of the tongue set ablaze.

The guards, as observers, are set upon interpretation and can have no sense of what it felt like as an experience; they focus on the why rather than the how. It would be "useless" now, as Paul recognizes, to put forward a practical explanation, that "my mount had stumbled, that I was pitched into a clump / of wild chamomile." The poem concludes on a poignant note, an understanding that transformation has its pathos for the individual yanked out of one identity into another: Saul, now on the road to becoming Paul, "would never enter" Damascus now as his old self. The transitions of visual perspectives in the poem mirror the social and narrative perspectives. Saul had been traveling in lofty disdain, with his head in the clouds, preoccupied with his important business; the sudden shift to ground level is a cultural jolt, his temporary blindness seems in part a response to a change of status, a sudden sense of vulnerability as much as a God-given affliction. The episode is replayed as physical and psychic trauma rather than revelation, which, as the opening lines ironically suggest, is the imaginative enhancement of the onlooker rather than the on the ground experience of the hapless victim. The last word of the poem, "home," is a surprising one, but it is a reminder of the security of being at home in an identity, however that might be constructed.

The final loss of identity in death is addressed in the last poem of the volume, "Old Folk's Home, Jerusalem." The question changes from what was seen, the preoccupation of "On the Road to Damascus," to "*How far off?*"—how long to the hour of death. Writing poetry seems irrelevant when life is reduced to physical indignity. The honeysuckle has a more "golden dotage" than the humans laid out in rows within these fortified Israeli settlements. Robert von Hallberg has noted how carefully this poem ghosts the sonnet form, never quite allowing itself those formal lyric consolations.[24] The final line, "Everyone waiting here was once in love," is a statement to line up with others in the volume. It cannot have the affirmation of the epigraph to "Obbligato" because it also acknowledges that love can be forgotten, but it does say, wryly, that love was in the picture somewhere at sometime, and it is a statement with the force of statement, albeit in the past tense, as the door of death stands "ajar."

Grace Notes began on Summit Beach with specifically African American constraints in relation to gender. The enlargement of opportunity for the descendants of the girl in the opening poem is charted autobiographically in the poems about Dove and her own daughter in which there is delight and determination to create a world for her "cream child" in a culture still, in many respects, a racist one. These are quintessentially American poems in their aspirational energies, drawing from the energies of Langston Hughes and Robert Hayden in their self-belief. Dove touches the grace notes of these lives, elliptically pondering their lost chances and their exemplary features, finding sainthood and savagery in American culture, noting wryly how individuals driven by the myths of American identity, create, in their distortions, their own extempore signature flourishes. The poet is, as always, searching for forms to convey the quality of lives, the few details, the notes, that admit their own status both as gleaned scraps but also recognize the universal narrative impulse, the impulse of individuals to latch onto an ideology that confers mythic destiny, "inventing their destinations" like the island women of Paris in order to create the grace notes of their existence. Dove honors, too, in her elliptical forms, the impulse of readers to find in the notes a narrative trajectory to amplify within their own imaginations.

The fascination of the shape of a life, whether famous or unknown, and the ideology that drives it, is the enlarging feature of this volume, which ranges geographically and historically, Jamesian in its curiosities and connections, if un-Jamesian in its brevities. That it is "a complex fate"[25] to be an American writer is a mantle that Dove wears as confidently as Henry James, with the same sense of internationalism and with a more searching sense as a black writer of what it means in terms of origins, the unstable "diaspora"[26] that constitutes America. The movement of *Grace Notes* is a movement forward from the limitations and dreams ("the tin roof into blue") of the opening poem, a movement into a critique of contemporary American culture in which personal autobiography is tempered by other lives, other cultures, and other times ("the Unbroken Blue" of Paul's sensation in "On the Road to Damascus"). There is harmony, scale, an extending, a showing forth of the individual note within the whole. In this true musical sense, the form of the volume is disclosed.

CHAPTER 6

Mother Love

Can You Hear the Pipes Playing?

Mother Love is a modern rendering of the classical myth of Demeter and Persephone, the story that expresses the metamorphic cycle of natural fertility, the seed germinated underground that, flowering in springtime and then decaying, returns seed to the earth for regeneration. Persephone, the daughter of Demeter, goddess of corn and fertility, picking flowers in a field with her friends, strayed apart from them. As she bent down to pluck a narcissus, the earth opened and Hades dragged her into his underworld kingdom to make her his queen. During her captivity, Persephone ate seven pomegranate seeds, an act that meant she would never be able to escape permanently. Meanwhile, Demeter, inconsolable, abandoned her duties as goddess responsible for agriculture and, disguised as a mortal, wandered the earth, grieving. Eventually, a bargain was made: Persephone was to spend part of the year underground with Hades, the other part with her mother on Earth.

Dove's own foreword to *Mother Love*, "An Intact World," gives a more detailed outline of the myth as she deploys it in her work and also acknowledges that her verse-cycle of seven sections, much of it in sonnet or near sonnet form, is "in homage and as counterpoint to Rilke's *Sonnets to Orpheus*."[1] The inconsolable loss of the loved one to the underworld and the desire to return her to Earth are common to the myths of Persephone and Orpheus. The son of Apollo, Orpheus was so marvelous a singer and musician that even nature listened entranced to him. He married Eurydice, a Naiad, who was pursued by Aristaeus in a field. In trying to escape, she was bitten by a snake and died. Orpheus charmed his way into the underworld to recover her. Hades and Persephone granted him the favor of being allowed to return with Eurydice to the upper world on condition that he led the way upward and did not look back to see if she was following. In the more tragic version of the myth, he could not resist looking back and therefore, through excess of love, lost her. The myths are thus intertwined and, in its expression of violation and loss, *Mother Love* both resists and allows the figure of Orpheus as lyric poet. In the patterning of contemporary voices, the notes of elegiac sweetness, of nature's thrum, are the Orphic trace.

The Written History

Part 1 of Dove's cycle has only one poem, "Heroes," which, apart from the title, seems to deny mythic resonance. It is not a sonnet but a laconic narrative of nine three-line stanzas with a single additional closing line. Nevertheless, one sharp-eyed critic, in tune with Dove's love of numerical puns, has noticed that this makes twenty-eight lines, the length of a double sonnet.[2] The vertical format of the poem is the story "starting to unravel," the irreversibility of the casual mundane action of picking a flower, from which follows unforeseen brutality, unreeling as if predestined and inescapable. Whereas in the myth, Persephone picks the flower, in this poem the perpetrator is not identified. By the title, it can be assumed to be a man, addressed throughout as "you," but it could be anyone, even the reader, who becomes entrapped in the consequences of a random act.

Picking the flower in the opening stanza, it is indeed as if we find ourselves in the myth unexpectedly, for although the action presumably springs from some kind of desire, there seems no urgency and the circumstances are unprepossessing:

> A flower in a weedy field:
> make it a poppy. You pick it.

The tone is flat and curiously ambiguous, for "make it a poppy" might be a creative command (bring a poppy into being) or an imperative (it must be a poppy) or, merely, that it might as well be a poppy as anything else. But a poppy does not come into a poem innocently. This fume-laden symbol, attribute of Demeter, suffused with sleep and death and, in modern iconography, redolent of the fields of war, of suffering and slaughter, can hardly make an inconspicuous entrance. The poppy, having been created, is picked. Again the tone is ambiguous: "You pick it" seems both a command and an idle response, but from this point onward, causality kicks in and the ironies unfold. The protagonist, in quest of water to revive the dying poppy, comes up against an angry woman for whom the poppy in the field (her garden) has been, ironically, a talisman against suicide. It is at this point that the language of the poem gets out of key with the events recounted. The language becomes more clichéd as the events become more bizarre and violent. It is as if the language can only "go through the motions" and recognizes its belatedness, its function as "the written history"[3] that the woman who is hit on the head by the protagonist "wouldn't live to read, anyway."

Dove creates a black comedy from the contrast between the out of control ugliness of events, "you strike her," and the narrative conferring order and inevitability. Roland Barthes has satirized the bogus authority of past tense in written narrative, how, in nineteenth-century fiction, this gives a spurious sense of order to events: "The world is not unexplained since it is told like a story; each one of its accidents is but a circumstance."[4] However, Dove, in this very concise narrative, with deliberate irony, imposes this causal clarity upon a *present-tense* sequence. The action "So you strike her" is endowed with clichéd inevitability, and "there's nothing to be done" glosses the panic-stricken reaction as the inevitable and only next step in the chain. The "written history" is posthumous, and the woman whose head is about to be pulped is offered a "juicy spot" in it by way of compensation. Well, if she does not seem to appreciate the offer, "she wouldn't live to read [it] anyway." The poem accelerates, as the protagonist, now a murderer, becomes a "fugitive." The self-rationalizing of the criminal converges with the narrowing down of possibility—"you have to," "you can't"—phrases that reverberate against the epigraph to part 1, "One had to choose, / and who would choose the horror?" The exasperated question at the end of the poem, "O why / did you pick that idiot flower?" in which "pick" is both choice and action, is answered mockingly and deliberately:

> Because it was the last one
> and you knew
>
> it was going to die.

The picking of the flower prefigures the woman's death and the fugitive's now more imminent sense of mortality. The narrative has unraveled itself as self-fulfilling prophecy, as a nasty little plot sprung upon the protagonist. The stony, low-key formality of "Heroes" has articulated a spectrum of violation from the minor ecological transgression of the opening to the enraged human encounter in which the mundane implodes unexpectedly out of control, in which, as the story line narrows down, the resonances spread like a stain of blood.

These resonances are not only moral and causal, the damaging encounters of humanity and nature, but also literary and mythic. This spare account only allows itself to come at the mythic obliquely, but its frame of reference is ambitious; the apparent simplicity of the poem is artful. The opening, "A flower in a weedy field," deliberately sets itself against other renditions of the myth. When Milton describes paradise in *Paradise Lost,* he leads into it through a series of images, one of which is the field in Dove's poem:

> Not that fair field
> Of Enna, where Proserpine gathering flowers
> Her self a fairer flower by gloomy Dis
> Was gathered, which cost Ceres all that pain
> To seek her through the world;[5]

A "weedy field" somewhere in the American Midwest seems a swerve away from Enna in Sicily, where the myth of Persephone's abduction was traditionally located. There are no paradisal connotations and no epic rhetorical enhancement in "Heroes." Nevertheless, Dove quotes from *Paradise Lost* in the epigraph to part 7, specifically locating her version of the myth in relation to Milton's. Paradise is already lost in "Heroes," the title of which rattles emptily against what happens to happen. Dove, like her older contemporary, John Ashbery, opts for a language resolutely flat and clichéd, yet (as also so often with Ashbery) the other language of tragic elevation is a trace that haunts the poem.

If the Miltonic is distant music, the Rilkean is a harmonic presence. In Rilke's *Sonnets to Orpheus,* the poet draws on a myth of masculine desire and loss. *Mother Love* is a feminine and feminist "counterpoint." These complementary perspectives fashion different versions of love yet also differing versions of creativity. Rilke, in taking the figure of Orpheus, feeds into and promulgates the myth of heroic artistry, the ecstasy of lyric creation. *Sonnets to Orpheus* begins:

> There arose a tree. O pure transcension!
> O Orpheus sings![6]

Rilke's second sonnet celebrates the coming into being of Eurydice: "She was almost a girl and forth she leaped / from this harmonious joy of song and lyre." As the sequence gets under way, poetic creativity is hailed as spontaneity, a beginning from which amplitude swells, a world of amazing fecundity.

Dove's world, in contrast, is planted with death, the poppy, and the speaker of the poem is skeptical about art creating a world of beauty: "make it" and "pick it" are not very Orphic choices or injunctions. Furthermore, the "jar" in the second stanza has the harshness of Wallace Stevens's "Anecdote of the Jar," itself a bleak refashioning of Keats's "Ode on a Grecian Urn." Stevens's anecdote instructs that the emblem of art, the jar," is "bare" and that it does "not give of bird or bush."[7] Art is not in Stevens's poem a Rilkean heroic activity of fabulous fecundity but a coldly ordering intrusion. The speaker of Dove's "Heroes," as artist-figure, is a knowing and ironic persona remote from the clumsy actions of the protagonist trying to "prop up the flower in the stolen jar." Yet the protagonist and his stolen jar are *also* emblems of the human impulse to aestheticize, itself a kind of violation of nature. To "pick" turns out not to be a clean act. Dove's poem acknowledges that we are burdened with guilt, with the Miltonic weight of expulsion from Paradise, acknowledges that art itself is the frail vessel in which we try to carry the wilting flower, nature, that we have ourselves despoiled. In part 2 of Rilke's *Sonnets to Orpheus,* the human weight of desire and creativity becomes more tragic and fateful:

> Look at the flowers, faithful to earth's ways,
> To whom we lend fate from fate's very rim—
> But who knows? If they grieve that they decay,
> We must be the grief for them.[8]

Rilke assigns to art an expressive voice speaking for nature in a high lyric mode of dignity and presence; for Dove, the "jar" of art is "stolen" from our contaminating interventions in nature. *Mother Love* expresses grief and loss but from the outset asserts that horror and violation in modern life are clichéd and banal.

Loss

Part 2 of *Mother Love* consists of twelve poems on the abduction of Persephone and Demeter's consequent grief. Just as classical versions of the myth slide between different persona, Persephone/Kora (meaning "girl"), so in this part, as throughout *Mother Love,* Persephone and Demeter are expressed in different forms and voices. There are other voices, too, often criss-crossing and modulating into one another. The modern voices are sometimes specifically African American, sometimes an impersonal narrating voice, sometimes the autobiographical presence of the poet herself; there are also the voices of Demeter and Persephone in more antique mode, as well as the impersonal voicing of nature's processes. The poems are formal in structure, many of them sonnets or variants of sonnets. Dove said that she liked "how the sonnet comforts even while its prim borders . . . are stultifying; one is constantly bumping up against Order."[9] The sequence opens by suggesting the life of an ordinary girl in a small-town American community. The contemporary idiom in the first poem, "Primer," evokes a world of "bobby socks" and bullying: one of the first real lessons of childhood is learning how to stand up for oneself. This Persephone's childhood is not idyllic, and the "Mother Goose" epigraph, the kind of folk rhyme that adults narrate to children, sets the tone: "If he hears you . . . / Limb from limb at once he'll tear you." Children are beset by mythologies inculcating fear, guilt, and curiosity.

Adolescence, in these pre-abduction poems, is a condenser of the will to be independent. The teenage speaker in the poem "Party Dress for a First Born" relegates the security of maternal love, like childhood, to the past. Her imagination is violent and erotic: her party dress is a "headless girl"; men at the party will "stride like elegant scissors." She is ready for the fray.

The sonnet "Persephone, Falling" invokes the myth more directly. In the octave, the girl strays, sees the narcissus, the flower so unlike the others—as she herself is picked out by destiny. However, she is an active agent in her fate. She doesn't gather the flower, but "pulled, / stooped to pull harder" and Hades claimed his due; she is lost. The sestet is an ironic chorus of the kinds of warnings that adults give to children, "Don't answer to strangers. Stick with your playmates." Yet the modern Persephone of these poems is wary and alert, enterprising and independent—not victim material. But disaster, like Hades, comes out of nowhere.

The group of poems about the aftermath of Persephone's disappearance expresses not only maternal grief and degradation but also the voice of the community, the choric urgings toward recovery. "The Search" is a modern version of Demeter's predicament after the loss of her daughter. In the myth, she leaves Olympus and wanders disconsolately. Her brother, Poseidon, god of sea and water, lusts after her, and although she takes the form of a mare to escape him, he (also traditionally associated with bulls and horses) takes equine shape and rapes her. In Dove's poem, the mother lets herself go, abandons cultural constraints, and, in giving way to nature, leaves herself vulnerable to casual bestiality. She becomes a down-and-out and is raped by the river. The community comments disapprovingly, "*Serves her right, the old mare.*" In replicating her daughter's violation, she enacts, in modern psychoanalytic terms, a form of guilt and self-abasement. Thus, with a temporal fluidity characteristic of the sequence as a whole, "The Search" fulfills the myth in a mode both psychological and communal.

The modern horror is abduction, disappearance without trace. The child speaker in the poem "Statistic: the Witness" is unable to expunge the images of the abduction from her consciousness, whereas "Persephone Abducted" is a reminder that horror also occurs in the vicinity of those who do not notice and do not hear the screams. The speaker of "Persephone Abducted," one of those who did not notice the crime, meditates upon the uselessness of philosophy or philosophical poetry after the event. Persephone cursed as she struggled, her features "withered" and haglike, but nearby those oblivious to her plight were "singing in the field." The poem implicitly acknowledges that lament is distanced from the ugliness of rage and terror. Indeed, what Dove called the "prim borders" of these near-sonnets are, at times, a prurient hedge against the jagged fragments embedded within.

The connections among sexuality, brutality, and fertility, for which the Persephone myth is both searing recognition and processing anodyne, are condensed in the poem "Protection." This is a racially inflected Demeter as an African American mother remembering her preoccupation with her daughter's "'good' hair" and questioning blues phrasing in "How done is gone?" The distraught Demeter sees her lost child's image in nature's growth and abundance: "Everywhere in the garden I see the slim vine / of your neck, the stubborn baby curls." Reminiscent of the fourth of Rilke's *Sonnets to Orpheus* in which "Those you planted as children"[10] become trees, Demeter's response is both acute personal memory and the beginning of acceptance. Acknowledgment of the process of merging into nature's cycle is a diffusion of the weight of grief. Yet there are still exasperated questionings: "Are you really all over with?" Metamorphosis and merging are alien to the crude demandings of the survivor. "The Narcissus Flower" is similarly metamorphic. Written from the perspective of the flower, the language slides into the imagery of masculine rape, "the earth unzipped," the "knife easing into / the . . . crevice," but a further metamorphosis in the human scenario is from fear to hate. Hatred is an assumption of regality for Persephone, as she becomes queen of the underworld.

"Grief: The Council," a key poem of part 2, is an antiphon of alternating voices. The first speakers are the voices of culture, a modern-day Greek chorus of African American women with a collective wisdom ranging from commonplace advice, "Get a hold on yourself," through exasperated frustration, "I bet she ain't took in a word I said," to responsibility, "I say we gotta see her through," and care, "Sister Jeffries, you could drop in / tomorrow." These gossipy voices chime antiphonally with italicized phrases that stray across them like tendrils of memory, as if nature rather than culture will assimilate and heal. The italicized passages are a reminder of Demeter's neglected duties as goddess of agriculture:

> I told her: enough is enough . . .
> > *to abdicate*
> > *to let the garden go to seed*

They are also a reminder that tending nature is assimilation, recovery, renewal, Persephone is in *"the kale's / green tresses, the corn's green sleeve,"* just as it is also loss and finality, *"no tender cheek nor ripening grape / destined for wine."* The final exchange between the human voices and the italicized more distant expression of the mythic workings of nature is beautifully accented:

> . . . Ain't this crazy weather?
> Feels like winter coming on.
>
> > *at last the earth cleared to the sea*
> > *at last composure*

The first voice expresses nature in disarray, and as in John Ashbery's poem "Crazy Weather," to speak about weather and landscape is also to speak about language. Ashbery recalls the time when the language of poetry

> came easily
> Through the then woods and ploughed fields and had
> A simple unconscious dignity we can never hope to
> Approximate now except in narrow ravines nobody

Will inspect where some late sample of the rare,
Uninteresting specimen might still be putting out shoots,
    for all we know.[11]

Dove, like Ashbery, commits herself to the "basic sunshine pour-
ing through," the communal babble, a language that is, in its
very platitudes, mythic. "Feels like winter coming on" acknowledges that Persephone is now in the underworld and "*at last
composure*" is the sign that Demeter and Poseidon, "earth" and
"sea," settle down to their tasks. The poem itself acquires a dignified composure from unlikely linguistic material. The clichéd
advice of the choric sections is a version of what Ashbery has
called "the proverbial disarray"[12] of our existence in language.
However, Dove, like Langston Hughes, knows how to start a
rhythm in simple repetitions, "I say . . . / I say," so that the
choric voices begin to hum. Eventually the romantic nature language and the African American gossips get on terms with each
other, "melting to a strings-and-sax ending."

"Mother Love," the title poem of the volume, an irregular
double sonnet, takes the interaction of the modern and the classical through the crucible of gender. It creates a tension between
contemporary cultural ideologies of gender (modern mythologies) and the deeper seam of the psychoanalytic-nature continuum that is expressed in traditional forms of myth. The first
stanza seems, initially, to be a celebration, a gathering up of all
the modern wisdom about motherhood: "Toss me a baby and
without bothering / to blink I'll catch her, sling him on a hip."
Yet the effect is mocking. It becomes evident that we are being
sold a masculine ideal of maternity: "duty bugles and we'll . . .
bare the nipple or tuck in the sheet." These internalizations of
the feminine role as approved by men are

> those one-way mirrors
> girls peer into as their fledgling heroes slip
> through, storming the smoky battlefield.

The modern woman is being sold a package that still leaves her holding the baby.

The second stanza, in classical mode, explores a more violent version of the Demeter myth that is keyed both to her desire for revenge and, paradoxically and understandably, her desire to erase human feeling. In this version of the story, Demeter disguises herself as an old woman. Resting by a well, she is approached by the four daughters of King Celeus and Queen Metanira and offered hospitality. Demeter, in gratitude, offers to serve in the royal household by caring for Queen Metanira's baby son Demophon. Demeter tries to make him immortal by anointing him with nectar by day and putting him on the fire at night to burn out his mortality.

If the first stanza is ironic about gender conditioning and the way "being needed" is the standard "remedy" for grief, the second stanza is more keenly ironic about the consequences of being "cured to perfection." The hapless male human baby "sizzling on a spit" is a comic revenge on the male species. There are uncomfortable historical resonances in the fact that this is a scene of torture in pursuit of a myth of perfectibility and cultural refashioning. History has shown that when humanity has "cured" itself of human feeling, the consequences have been terrible. The poem, however, remains decisively in the comic vein, in sync with Demeter's own batty remark, "Oh, I know it / looked damning." Only humans with their imperfections would think so. Even Demeter carries some residual memory of feeling:

> Poor human—
> to scream like that, to make me remember.

The effect of the poem is, indeed, caustic. The challenge to modern gender stereotypes, to the ways women are taught to nurture, is succeeded by a Swiftian satiric exposé of a world "cured" of feeling. The poem metamorphoses seamlessly from one to the other through a gossipy bridge, "So when this kind woman approached," as if this was a seamless transition. It is something of an achievement to have written a poem called "Mother Love" without a whiff of sentiment and with such a fine-honed double consciousness. To read it intertextually with Rilke's *Sonnets to Orpheus* brings the achievement into relief. Rilke, in the early sonnets of the sequence, is preoccupied with the idea that only the poet who, like Orpheus, has inhabited the underworld and has eaten with the dead, can express the other world:

> Only in the dual
> realm will voices become
> eternal and pure[13]

Dove is frequently drawn to doubling and antiphonal voices in her parallels between the mythic and the modern, but rather than seeking the "eternal and pure," her intent is to sharpen differing ideological positions. Lyric impulse is checked by a determination to retain the grittiness of the dual realm.

Indeed, part 2 closes with two poems in a brittle contemporary idiom. In "Breakfast of Champions," Demeter, returned home after her wanderings, pours out her breakfast cereal. She is making some kind of recovery in the approved American style.

"Golden Oldie," the final poem, turns on the haunting banality of a phrase from a sixties song, "Baby, where did our love go?"[14] a phrase "crooned / by a young girl dying to feel alive."

Culture and Nature

Part 3 of *Mother Love,* "Persephone in Hell," a poem in seven sections (an equivalent of the seven pomegranate seeds eaten by Persephone) is set in the underworld, which turns out to be Paris, every anxious mother's city of the damned. It reveals Persephone as an American college girl intent on having fun away from home. She cruises for adventure, thrilled with the "instantly foreign," setting an exacting standard of amusement, wanting to go beyond expatriate parties, yet the refrain mocks her American pursuit of happiness:

> *are you having a good time*
> *are you having a good time at all*

Paris is more of a wintry wasteland of dog shit and "gutters, dry rivers of the season's detritus," a Baudelairean miasma,[15] than a thrilling encounter with sin. In the fourth section, Persephone finds herself by the Pompidou Center,[16] struggling with the "iron breath of winter." An italicized choric voice expresses the scenario: "*This is how the pit opens.*" The Pompidou, "throbbing with neon tubing / like some demented plumber's diagram," is an appropriate figure for the irritants afflicting the arid soul. The poem is an X ray of the state of desolation. "The Persephone in Hell" sequence, as a whole, audits the discomforts of T. S. Eliot's *Waste Land.*[17] In the exasperated spirit of the prior poem, it trawls the modern metropolis. The terrain is brittle, urban modernity in its crude jumbling of "banjos" and "bad sculpture." But this contemporary superstructure cannot suppress the marshy exhalations of myth that seep through in the fateful choric voice:

> *This is how one foot*
> *sinks into the ground*

The stage is set: Persephone is ready to be caught. The encounter with Hades is cued in the fifth section, an interior monologue by this bored middle-aged Parisian painter in need of a "divertissement." As a stimulus to his jaded sensibility, Hades decides to pursue the next person who emerges from the escalator of the Metro. By an ironic twist of the legend, Persephone comes from *below* ground to encounter Hades at street level. Section 6, the meeting, reveals how their different agendas happen to require each other at this point. The interplay of interior consciousness and conversation is adroitly structured to convey the banality of the encounter, its apparatus of illusions, its status as "*un mirage,*" the frisson of recognition, "*Here you are,*" and the seductive routine, "I lift the glass, / lift to meet his." The scene is more often perceived through Persephone's eyes and she is less the victim than a quick-witted contender. Branding Hades a "cynical parrot," she notes how "his enquiry / curls down to lick my hand," and then she interrupts and completes his explanation of chartreuse. It is all very brittle and contemporary, but the mode changes in the seventh and last section of part 3. This, like the call and response of blues phrasing, is a chiming mythic antiphon of one-line phrases in which Persephone and Hades,[18] in their "cold longing," embrace, "sinking through heat" into nature. The poem can be read as two parallel vertical poems (each of fourteen lines and thus slim-line sonnets), the left-hand justified column of phrases for Persephone's voice and the right-hand column of phrases for Hades. It can also be read horizontally across the page so that it becomes antiphonal, cry and response, the personal subsumed into the cycle of nature, the earth drawing down the seed into its darkness.

It is characteristic that Dove pulls the myth into the contemporary, with the freight of the modernist metropolis, but with something beyond the modernist ennui and the diffidence and disgust that is a feature of contemporary sexual relationships in *The Waste Land*. The sexual encounter in "Persephone in Hell" is not, however, a grand passion but an erotic game with all manner of cultural interfaces to be negotiated. These contemporary elements are in the ascendancy, yet they metamorphose without gradation into the classical. Mythology, in *Mother Love,* is thus at once the earth's cycle, the sensual heat of eroticism, but also the cultural rite of passage, the mother deserted for the lover, and the antique and the contemporary compacted within nature's drive.

Part 4, five additional poems set in Paris, is a witty expression of the accommodations that culture has to make with nature. It begins with "Hades' Pitch," a sonnet expressing the seduction of Persephone. The title puns on the colloquialism, his pitch or play for her, and his black-as-pitch, dastardly intent. As seducer, he is cunning, urgent, and slightly pathetic. Persephone, in her American college girl persona, is not an innocent virgin: she "considers" Hades' proposition and decides to comply, seduced more by his language than by his physical presence. In the closing sestet of the sonnet, her sexual surrender in the underworld of the Parisian demimonde occurs at the same moment as, above ground, her mother the goddess Demeter is raped by her brother Poseidon. In Dove's version of the mythology, Demeter's rape is symbolic of the cultural rite of passage, the loss of her daughter: mother and daughter are both "bereft in an instant" of their exclusive relationship, a double phallic wounding.

Not a tragic event, though, hardly even momentous for the modern Persephone in whose mind, in the poem *"Wiederkehr"* (meaning "recurrence" or "repetition"), the seduction rapidly becomes a confining relationship. She figures out Hades' male chauvinism and resists his desire to find renewal in her youth. When the opportunity comes, she leaves. But the effect of the experience is to make her feel homesick so that she invites her mother for a visit. The lunch date meeting of mother and daughter in the final poem of part 4, a longer poem aptly titled "The Bistro Styx," is primarily registered through the cynical yet anxious maternal consciousness. Here Demeter is a sophisticated woman registering every detail of her daughter's new style of dress. Their guarded dialogue is conducted amid the rituals of Parisian cuisine that are, with comic irony, accorded a high French seriousness. Utterly contemptuous of the middle-aged Hades as the seducer who has persuaded her daughter to pose nude for his "appalling canvases," Demeter is nevertheless determined to observe the social protocols, as her daughter eats her way through a large meal. Persephone bites into a fig (a version of the seven seeds of the pomegranate) and seals her fate: by the act of eating in the underworld, she can never be entirely free from it. The cycle of her existence in the myth as part of the year below ground and part on the earth is now set in process. Recognizing *"I've lost her,"* Demeter pays the bill.

The Blues

In part 5, the perspective is contemporary, at times blues in spirit or, more loosely, in a blue mood. The speaker is often the persona of the poet herself, reflecting on the variations on male chauvinism or her own female submission to nature's cycle in menstrual rhythm, the seemingly unchangeable intrusions of nature into culture and culture into nature. The opening poem, "Blue Days," turns on a crude truckers' joke about women tracking slime. For the poet, hearing this, not surprisingly, diminishes the sensory gusto of a "halcyon" summer day. Nothing much has changed on the male chauvinism front over the centuries. The poet speaks ironically to Demeter: add this one to your "basket / of mysteries." In "Nature's Itinerary," the poet again adds her own jaundiced voice to the criss-crossing of voices in *Mother Love*. Traveling and altitude (attending an international poetry conference in Mexico) disrupt the poet's contraceptive-controlled monthly rhythm. Nature reasserts herself. Dove's disorientation and restless transit is a version of Demeter's disconsolate wanderings and Persephone's transient sojourns. In locating the mythic displacements in the modern, such displacements can be embraced. As in Dove's earlier volumes, *Mother Love* posits travel, the transitional, as the contemporary mode of life. Unlike her mythic forebears, the poet has the freedom to choose her journeys.

That such freedoms might be won out of suffering is the theme of "Sonnet in Primary Colors." The blues, originating in African American vernacular expression, are in Ralph Ellison's words, an "autobiographical chronicle of personal catastrophe expressed lyrically."[19] The blues impulse, as Ellison also noted, is to squeeze art from suffering. The poem brings the Mexican painter Frida Kahlo into the blues orbit, acknowledging her

bodily pain (the corset for her spinal injury) and her tempestu-
ous relationship with her partner, painter Diego Rivera, yet also
her indomitable creative spirit, her paintings as votive offerings
to God. Kahlo's paintings, based on folk idioms and impelled by
her socialist ideals and religious visions, were garishly colored,
powerful assertions of belief. Kahlo, who was handed out only
pain, "painted herself a present." This is a kind of antidote to
the preoccupation of the section with grief and with nostalgia
for the past. Kahlo painted herself a "present" not only in the
sense of a gift but also in the sense of not dwelling on misfor-
tune, not living in the past. In contrast, Persephone and Demeter, in mythic guise, are consumed by the other life of the past.
"Demeter Mourning" reveals Demeter as inconsolable, living a
kind of afterlife of the senses. More poignantly, in "Afield" she
watches her daughter walking in the meadow as if trying to
return to Hades. Demeter's perception is not only mythic, the
mother sensing the pull of the fateful cycle, the rhythm of
nature, but also feminist in the contemporary sense. In the sestet, she recognizes how women internalize patriarchal attitudes.
This is also a reminder that, in the classical story, when Demeter protested against Persephone's abduction, Zeus, although he
disapproved, allowed it. The final word of the poem, "putres-
cence"—in gender terms expressive of corrupt ideology—also
links back to the violence of the first poem, "Heroes." Growth
emanates from disorder and violence: "earth's ignorant flesh,"
in its fecundity, feeds off putrefaction.

Part 5 concludes with "Lost Brilliance," Persephone's nostalgic reminiscence of her regal underground status as Hades' con-
sort. In this poem, the memory of her capture is of drowning,
alluding to a version of the myth located in Sicily in which
Hades' chariot drags her underwater. More potently, it recalls

the Styx, the river of classical legend, in which the souls of the dead were conveyed to the underworld by Charon, the boatmen. Persephone remembers the journey, how "his oars sighed / up to the smoking shore." This elegiac austerity expressed in shades of gray (like her costume in "The Bistro Styx") is punctuated with crimson, "all that marble / flayed with the red plush of privilege," the miseries and splendors of captivity. The poem winds down, in the final shorter lines, to the enslavement of erotic obsession:

> and then there was just
> the two of us forever:
> one who wounded,
> and one who served.

This self-consuming passion, operatically played out in a "Venetian / palazzo" replete with hell fire (a setting reminiscent of Joseph Losey's 1979 film of Mozart's *Don Giovanni*), metamorphoses into a modern abusive relationship. Yet this has been an initiatory rite into sexuality. Whatever Hades has taken, he has conferred a physical self upon Persephone.

The "traveling," the restlessness that is a keynote of *Mother Love*, indicative of its preoccupation with changing states, with metamorphosis, infects the characters not only with the desire to move beyond the present state but also with a longing to recover an earlier phase that will somehow bring them a beginning again. This is true not only for Demeter but also, in a more complicated way, for Persephone, who had her own kind of power over her middle-aged lover, withholding her youthful "rain" from him and then leaving him when it became monotonous and at times hankering to exert that power again. The feminism of *Mother Love* is not primarily a critique of patri-archy. Hades in his modern guise is not particularly wicked, and cultural manipulation is revealed as characteristic of both sexes. Such manipulations in themselves reveal culture as subordinate to nature. The cycle of nature, the seasons, the phases of human life, to which all characters must accede, is one of the structur-ing rhythms of *Mother Love*. This rhythm, elliptically revealed in phrases here and there, nevertheless disturbs and rearranges cultural identity. The human effort to place a cultural template over Earth's momentum is dislocated and fragmentary. Dove herself said that she afterward realized that an unconscious motive for choosing the Demeter-Persephone myth must have been that "my daughter Aviva was about five years old at the time, just about to enter kindergarten, to go out into the world. I had some adjustment to do as a mother."[20] Nature, however culturally imprinted, will have its sway. Dove writes, too, of "mother-goddess, daughter-consort and poet" as "struggling to sing in their chains."[21] *Mother Love* is a rueful confession that nature's enchaining of the female slews the feminist desire to take control.

The structure of the volume, taking bits and pieces of myth, slotting them into snippets of the contemporary, shuttling between Paris and the United States, between the metropolitan and the rural, between Pompidou and pastoral, undermines ideas of human control. The contemporary voices are no more in charge than the classical. Indeed, transitions between classical and modern often occur several times within one poem. As in *Thomas and Beulah,* Dove deploys the lyric fragment, but in *Mother Love* it is deployed in a more dislocated mode. *Mother Love* is built on oppositions and contrasts that are frequently breached. It expresses the cycle of nature and its classical mythic pastoral representation, against which are built the "knowing" voices of culture, choric or individual, most often urban and modern. Intrusively juxtaposed, combined, then disconnected, neither of these two modes is allowed continuous expression. This denial of a secure narrative base echoes the instability of the large two-phase structure of the myth (Persephone's underground and above ground existences). The reader from the beginning is kept on the stretch: jolted into the contemporary, seduced by the lyricism of mythic pastoral, and amused by some incongruous fusion of the two but not allowed to habituate, to naturalize in any mode. In "Demeter, Waiting," the goddess, refusing in her grief to go about her agricultural duties, speaks in a querulous contemporary idiom: "I will wail and thrash / until the whole goddamned golden panorama freezes / over." Tragic mythic narrative is comically deflated by the modern colloquial. Yet these different generic elements and shifts of voice are brought together into a whole.

Is there music in these disjunctions? Are there motifs that link these disparate elements? Is this a harmonious polyphony? Dove's choice of epigraph to part 6 of *Mother Love*, from Muriel Rukeyser's "The Poem as Mask," suggests that these fissures and fragments *are* the whole. Orpheus, god of music and poetry, is the speaker in Rukeyser's poem. Orpheus initially talks confidently of assuming masks but then repudiates this, confessing that this was no distancing device, but that when he wrote, it was "myself split open." His declaration, "No more masks! No more mythologies!" paradoxically liberates him into artistic power in the concluding lines that Dove chose for her epigraph:

> Now, for the first time, the god lifts his hand,
> the fragments join in me with their own music.[22]

The composing, godlike power of art stems from "torn life." Only then can the conductor lift his baton, can the "fragments join in me." This is very carefully phrased and even more exact in the continuation, "with their own music," suggesting not only that the fragments are artistically distinctive but also that they are the parts of the score *and* the musicians in the orchestra. For Dove, the epigraph enhances her artistic belief in the potency of the fragment. Myth is seductive in that it invites us to read nature as enlarged human experience, as if with an organic sense of the self, as if the self is made whole by its performance of the larger rhythms in which it is in fact only a small fragment. Wary of that seduction, Dove is also faithful to the chaotic aspects of individual human submission to nature, faithful to the way that experience does not make sense.

With such saturation in the potentiality of the mythic, *Mother Love* is less preoccupied with history than Dove's other collections, but part 6 of the volume expands the myth into political and historical dimensions. It draws attention to the recurrence throughout human existence of imprisonment, enslavement, and loss and the ways in which literature and art have come out of those circumstances. The opening poem, "Political," is dedicated to Breyten Breytenbach, an Afrikaner poet and political dissident who "spent seven years in hell's circles." Imprisoned for treason in South Africa in 1975, the first two years of his seven behind bars were in solitary confinement. The relationship of slavery and art is ironically noted in the formal sonnet "Teotihuacán," which features a group of twentieth-century poets on a guided tour of the ancient pyramid site near Mexico City. They are shown how Aztec slaves ground up tiny bugs collected from cactus plants to make the red color for decorating the Temple of the Sun: "it took millions of those bugs to stain a single wall." Nature has thus become transmuted into cultural stain. The modern tourist-poets, scribbling in their notebooks, are curious but detached. The delineation of enslavement in "Teotihuacán" is deliberately distanced: the poet records how she and other poets recorded the information. This is history from the outside, tagged as a masculine way of explaining, whereas in the poem "History," a pregnant woman imagines it as if from the inside. The coolness of "Teotihuacán" contrasts with the "wail and thrash," the immediacy of frustration and pain in "Demeter, Waiting." Yet in part 6, change is underway. Demeter gets weary of grief. In a number of poems, her language is coarse and colloquial, a sign of renewal of energy. Eventually she decides to get on with life. In the poem "Rusks," in the role of a blues singer, she comes round to accepting "half a happiness," declaring, "Let someone else have / the throne of blues for a while."

Demeter's language of loss and recovery in parts 5 and 6 is frequently in this crude demotic "itch" and "scratch," "wail and thrash." She delivers cliché and platitude with an aplomb that shows she is getting better. The title, "Demeter's Prayer to Hades," might suggest linguistic decorum, a reverential acceptance of the new order, but it has a sting in its tail. Advising Hades with what seems like an all-American piety, "Believe in yourself, / go ahead," her apparent encouragement is, in fact, cynical—"see where it gets you." However, this robust language, future-directed, a feature of a number of poems, is shadowed by the ghostly presence of the past. The poem "Missing" alludes to the conclusion of Toni Morrison's novel *Beloved*,[23] as it closes with a poignant evocation of the trace of the loved one: "I am the one that comes and goes; / I am the footfall that hovers."

That there is a time to turn to the world again is expressed in the formal injunctions of the poem "Lamentations," which draws on the pastoral tradition. Orpheus's music, in whatever form, here the pipes of shepherds, is a consolation to be grasped, an expression of our nature, of our fullness in the world *now* that should not be refused. The beauty of the lines has a quiet authority:

> Throw open the shutters
> to your darkened residences:
> can you hear the pipes playing,
> their hunger shaking the olive branches?
> To hear them sighing and not answer
> is to deny this world,

It is significant, though, that in this sonnet of abbreviated lines, the "silken / air" of lyric expression is only allowed the octave and that in the sestet the "brute tongue" of a common-sense voice takes over.

Nature and Form

Part 7, the concluding section of *Mother Love,* is "Her Island," an extended crown of sonnets in which the closing line of each one becomes the opening line of the next. The sonnets in this section are the most orthodox of the volume, varying between thirteen and fifteen lines, sometimes divided into two parts, with only occasional variations in line length. That is to say they look almost like traditional sonnets. The classic formality of the structure plays against but also echoes, in its circularity, the frustration of the experience conveyed. The sonnets trace Dove's search for the ruins of Demeter's temple near Agrigento on the island of Sicily. The quest is tedious; the poet-tourist, contending with summer heat and the garbage with which contemporary culture pollutes nature, feels herself unlikely to be on epiphanic ground. The epigraph to part 7, from Milton's *Paradise Lost,* in which Satan, "the lost Arch Angel," contemplates the "Region" to which he is consigned, having lost the "celestial light" of "Heav'n," sets the idiom of dereliction and belatedness.

Agrigento seems, to Dove, a similarly hellish region, "stricken with sirocco": "nothing will come of this / textbook rampaging." Demeter's grotto is disappointing, but the poet and her husband do find an old man who offers to guide them across town to an overgrown temple of Vulcan, god of fire. Later they find other fragments of temples, "exalted litter" all over the island. The questing tourists are also bent on finding the lake in the center of the island said to have been created where the nymph, Cyane, witnessing Persephone's abduction, in her grief, melted into water. They find the lake surrounded by a modern "racetrack," "no cave, no reeds." Hades' chariot has been transformed into racing cars; the mythic pastoral scene cannot be found. Modern Sicily is the macho world of fast driving, political corruption, and violence, with car bombs blowing up judges who worked to bring the Mafia to justice. Yet in part 7, the poet and her husband unobtrusively represent a companionable husband-and-wife model of modern sexual relations that exists alongside the mythic tale of violation and loss and alongside the modern culture that litters the landscape, obliterating yet repeating the past.

The opening sonnet of "Her Island" situates the poet and her husband in Sicily searching for Demeter's temple: it begins "Around us: blazed stones, closed ground." This expresses the inhospitable nature of the terrain, its refusal to give up secrets.

However, the closing line of the last sonnet in the cycle (the last poem in the volume) repeats this line in slightly different form: "around us: blazed stones, the ground closed." That final phrase, "the ground closed," alters the balance of meaning. The poetic imagination has mined the ground (however unpromising it has been at times) and chooses to close now. The "blazed stones" represent inscription, the imagination's mark and trace, both past and present. There is recognition, too, that "no story's ever finished." The poet and her husband, exhausted in the heat, leaning on the earth, the "wild / mother we can never leave," acquiesce in the earth's narrative "all / around us." The enclosing form of the crown of sonnets acknowledges that humans are enclosed within the cycle of nature.

The Mythical Method

The achievement of *Mother Love* is to give late twentieth-century poetic expression to what T. S. Eliot, writing about James Joyce's novel, *Ulysses,* called the "mythical method," the ability to manipulate a "continuous parallel between contemporaneity and antiquity."[24] In Eliot's own poem of 1922, this compacting of the contemporary and the antique is particularly evident in relation to gender and sexuality. In spite of the androgynous figure of Tiresias, *The Waste Land* is written from a masculine perspective, from a sense of masculinity uncertain and undermined. It is essentially a masturbatory text: dry wrestlings leak yearnings and self-loathings; crabbed pedantic scuttlings impose a scholarly carapace upon romantic despair and desuetude. This is what gives the poem its sour odor, its authority as an expression and as an exposé of a masculine malaise. Eliot, publishing in the aftermath of the carnage of the

First World War, was acute in his realization that a certain kind of heroic masculinity was, in that climate, a dismantled literary topic. As if in furious denial, one strand of American writing thereafter, from Ernest Hemingway through Norman Mailer to Cormac McCarthy, relentlessly pursued myths of masculinity in search of something at once primal yet spectacularly culturally coded as American. Eliot's location of heroic masculinity in a mythic past, his representation of masculine diminishment in the wasteland of contemporary Europe, was a model that his successors did everything to repudiate.

A preoccupation with gender is similarly at the heart of Dove's "mythic method." Animated by an understanding that myth is not only nature in its human mask but also that myth is nature encoded by culture, she draws on and turns around the masculine narrative of the urban *flaneur*,[25] the male gaze in its cosmopolitan mode. Persephone is the American girl as *flaneuse*, curious rather than diffident, going about her "complex fate"[26] in Europe. This is not only to say that Persephone has literary predecessors, but that Dove, like Eliot, knows that it is necessary to realign earth and city, nature and culture. Like Eliot, too, in her revaluations of gender relationships, she is aware that old brutalities persist in new guises.

Dove ironically demonstrates that the banality of evil surfaces in any field to become the stuff of modern media attention, the "trumpeting kiosk's tales of odyssey and heartbreak" ("Wiring Home"). Her waste land is not only Paris, not only European, but also American, although here there is, as a steadying counterweight, the small-town community consoling Demeter with "Mason jars" and "movies" ("Grief: The Council"). Whereas Eliot ranges from the mock-heroic to comic doggerel in his expression of the banality of contemporary existence,

Dove, in *Mother Love,* is comfortable with the banal and presses it into service. Demeter is thus not only Mother Earth grieving for her lost daughter but, at the same time, our contemporary, subject to and subjecting readers to the idiolect of sex and shopping. Whether or not we like it, that used language, the language of cliché, is the expression of the human community. Demeter's choice, our choice, is between anomie, disintegration, or acceptance of that language, culture's rough and ready embrace.

Nevertheless, *Mother Love* is not only a cool analysis of customary language, not just John Ashbery with a cold compress. Neither is it merely a revisiting of choric values in the African American community. For it is also an agent of change; its theme is metamorphosis. The roles of violator and violated are paraded and parodied, played and replayed in recognition that these overrehearsed lines are the "written history," the way it has been and thus the way it has been recorded. But *Mother Love* is not a monument. The poet's passionate quest for mythic origin is a search to underwrite a new sense of feminine identity, one that will give due weight to that which pulls women to the earth.[27] Dove acknowledged Rilke's *Sonnets to Orpheus* as inspiration, but the affinity is more than formal. Rilke's sonnet sequence was largely composed in 1922, the same year as the publication of Eliot's *The Waste Land.* Unlike Eliot, Rilke's sensibility was attuned to the possibility of the feminine as the catalyst for change. *Sonnets to Orpheus* was occasioned by the death of a young girl, a dancer whom he, in fact, hardly knew, but it gave him the opportunity for lyric celebration of the feminine. In a letter of this period, Rilke's extraordinary prescience about historic shifts of gender understanding seems apposite to Dove's preoccupation with metamorphosis. Its importance deserves extensive quotation:

The girl and the woman, in their new, their own unfolding, will but in passing be imitators of masculine ways, good and bad, and repeaters of masculine professions. After the uncertainty of such transitions it will become apparent that women were only going through the profusion and vicissitude of those (often ridiculous) disguises in order to cleanse their own most characteristic natures of the distorting influences of the other sex. Women, in whom life lingers and dwells more immediately, more fruitfully and more confidently, must surely have become fundamentally riper people, more human people, than easygoing man, who is not pulled down below the surface of life by the weight of any fruit of his body, and who, presumptuous and hasty, undervalues what he thinks he loves. This humanity of women, borne its full time in suffering and humiliation, will come to light when she will have stripped off the conventions of mere femininity in the mutations of her outward status. . . . Some day there will be girls and women whose name will no longer signify merely an opposite of the masculine, but something in itself, something that makes one think, not of any complement and limit, but only of life and existence: the feminine human being.[28]

Rilke's subject in *Sonnets to Orpheus* is metamorphosis, how lament can become praising. In *Mother Love,* the epigraphs to the seven parts of the volume gesture to the darker side of the cycle. In this aspect and in others, Dove is working, to quote her phrase, "as counterpoint" to Rilke. Whereas his imagery is of flowing and breathing, flight and music, Dove's poems are connected across the volume not only by the earth and flowers (flowers that humans pick) but also by the slime trail of dirty jokes, by dog shit, flies, and detritus, as if we have to open our eyes to the messy propinquity of dream and dross. In "Demeter's Prayer to Hades," Demeter alludes to Adam's naming and inscribing the animals and plants of the Garden of Eden and, by implication, links this to Hades' act of appropriation. This might seem on the way to forgiveness, except that, like Eve to Adam, Demeter wishes upon Hades the knowledge that she has acquired of dream metamorphosing to dereliction:

> Now for the first time
> I see clearly the trail you planted,
> what ground opened to waste,
> though you dreamed a wealth
> of flowers.

Dove counterpoints Rilke's consolatory "Don't fear to suffer pain; / give the heaviness back to earth's weight again"[29] with the more Miltonic weight of all our woe in that "ground opened to waste." But her verse is Rilkean in the erotic pressure of the earth. In the final sonnet, Demeter's "deepest / dread" is that "her child could drown in sweetness." This is a sensual music, "silken / air and brute tongue," seductive and urgent:

> can you hear the pipes playing,
> their hunger shaking the olive branches?

CHAPTER 7

On the Bus with Rosa Parks
Living History

After the mythic world of *Mother Love,* Rita Dove's next volume, *On the Bus with Rosa Parks,* declares by its title an engagement with American democratic history as shaped by African Americans (the volume spans from 1925 to 1999). *Cameos,* the opening cycle of short poems, revisits the world of *Thomas and Beulah,* reaffirming the experience of ordinary black Americans as poetic subject. This backward glance at a traditional family is not, however, nostalgic but connective. It serves as a prelude to the poems that express how these same kind of ordinary people became politically active. During the period she was poet laureate (1993–95), Dove reiterated her commitment to the "underside of history":

> I remembered what my American history textbooks had reported and what they had chosen to ignore. The fascination with the underside of history—its vanquished and oppressed peoples, its ordinary citizens and unsung heroes—has accompanied me ever since.[1]

The characters in *Cameos* are the predecessors of those in the next generation, like Rosa Parks, whose resistance to segregation laws in the 1950s and 1960s made history, not only black history but also American history. As black women claiming civil rights, they changed the larger culture by declaring "Lady

Freedom among Us" (to quote the title of a poem central to this volume). In Martin Luther King's words, it was these "disinherited children of God" who "sat down at lunch counters" and refused to "ride segregated buses" who "were in reality standing up for what is best in the American dream."[2] In the poem "Lady Freedom among Us," as in the collection as a whole, Dove situates black achievement not as separatist but as "among" the diversity of people and regions, all the "us" that make up the United States.

On the Bus with Rosa Parks looks not only to recent American history but also to past centuries. History is preoccupied with units of time and the volume has its share of end-of-century and end-of-millennium thoughts. Closure invites recall and return. The section, *Revenant,* counterpoints autobiographical reflection with a sense of the past as visitant and visitable. In "Ghost Walk," a chateau is haunted by a ghost returning to past happiness, but in the title poem of the section, "Revenant," the spectacle of state punishment is a sight from which a visiting angel flees. This is a volume that, suspended between old and new, takes stock, personally and culturally. For all that it reaches back into European history, the "*living* history"[3] of this journey is primarily American. The title, *On the Bus with Rosa Parks,* expresses not only the civil rights journey (still in process) but also the life journey, the movement forward, the panorama glimpsed as it recedes, already, from view. Aside from its political and racial connotations, the bus is a homely vehicle, and to make a bus (popularly derided as a "loser-cruiser") rather than the automobile the image of the American journey is to restate the terms, to acknowledge communality rather than libertarian independence as a key American value.

Cameos

Cameos represents an elliptical history of an African American family in the fifteen years from 1925 to 1940. Each of the ten poems has a few sensory details picked out of a larger context, like a figure in relief upon a different colored ground in a cameo stone. Furthermore, these are pattern poems—the very precise visual shapes enhance the potency of the individual stanza as a distilled narrative segment.

If there is precision, there is also heat in the first poem, "July, 1925," which exudes sexuality and sentimentality in expressing the plight of Lucille, the African American woman, pregnant, as fecund as the vegetation in the garden around her, but abandoned by her man. The visual scenario consists of Lucille, the birdbath decorated with plastic flamingos, and the vine of green tomatoes. The tableau quality of such an image is, nevertheless, replete with narrative. The narrative is doubly accented: a dry, laconic omniscient statement such as "Lucille among the flamingos / is pregnant" is in counterpoint to the expression of Lucille's own fatalistic consciousness yearning for the return of her errant man. The green tomato that Lucille cannot stoop to reach on the vine is the symbol of the domestic tranquility she desires to create from her unpropitious circumstances. She wants to take the tomato and to "fry / the tart and poison out." If she obtains the tomato, Joe will come back. The narrator's comment at the end of the second stanza, "Inconsiderate, then," as if in disapproval of Joe's behavior, is also a comic reproof to the objects for their tactlessness in drawing attention (by their intrusive pathetic fallacy) to Lucille's parlous situation:

Inconsiderate, then,

the vine that languishes

so!, and the bath sighing for water
while the diffident flamingos arrange
their torchsong tutus.

The reader of *Thomas and Beulah* cannot help but be reminded of the bleak final poem of the sequence, "The Oriental Ballerina," in which the ballerina symbolizes all the things that Beulah has dreamed of but not achieved. But Lucille's desires are more home-centered and immediate: the happy omen of the tomato plopping into her hand transforms the flamingos into a "cloud" of "blossoming flame." There is a comic extravagance in her optimism and she is, in any case, in the full summer of adult life not, as with Beulah, near the end.

Dove's originality in "July, 1925," as in *Cameos* generally, is to invest blues phrasing with a modernist fastidiousness in laying down the line. This is an old, banal story of the abandoned woman, laid out, phrase separated from phrase, with lines ending or suspending in conscious artistry. The wit of the poem lies in its readiness to inhabit the borderline between pathos and bathos, to luxuriate unabashedly in the fecundity of language in a mean context. The tomato that falls into Lucille's hand is "plump" and "tart," like her own destiny.

Whereas the mood of "July, 1925" is passive feminine yearning, the second poem, "Night," from the perspective of the recalcitrant roaming Joe, follows a stereotypical masculine track. The enjambment wittily slips to reveal him as hostage to lust, not responsibility, as the line "No wonder he couldn't leave" turns into the next line, "her be." Joe could desert her, but he could not resist her. The narrative progression of Joe's altogether standard behavior (for a man whose absentee father was the model of the masculine role), succinctly balances self interest and contrition in the sequence that leads to his going home:

> Joe
> in funk and sorrow, Joe
> in parkbench celibacy, in apostolic
> factory rote,

Lucille and Joe represent the age-old feminine and masculine agendas displayed but also empathized. Lucille, in her Garden of Eden, has the green tomato falling as carnal knowledge, lush and tart; Joe, "apostolic" (the apostolics were a heretical sect who wandered about without shoes, bags, or money in imitation of the apostles) survivor of "factory rote," at least, like a homing pigeon, has return imprinted in his genes. The lives of Lucille and Joe are hard yet inwardly mobile. Within the cultural patterns laid down by era, race, and class, they exist in a physicality that is succinctly yet intensely rendered. The imaginative interest of *Cameos* is not so much in how these gender roles are constructed as in how they are vividly inhabited.

The sequence of poems shows the new baby, their first boy, cosseted by his myriad sisters through the Depression years. Like a young Coriolanus, he smashes flies and moodily plots escape from petticoat government. His aspirations are, for the family, only to be expected from a male and thus deserving of upper case reverence: "As It Should Be." The destiny of a girl is "to wait / her Turn." The spirit of the sequence is light and nonjudgmental in the witty placing of the thoughts of the family members, poignantly bound by the opening image of nature that requires nurture to make it palatable, the green tomato that needs (to recall Lucille's thoughts in the opening poem) to be cooked to "fry / the tart and poison out."

Joe, at his son's graduation, conscious that his offspring has no time for him, thinks of the filial ripening as "quiet / poison on a / shelf." The recurrence of the image is a kind of poetic justice for Joe's own youthful irresponsibility. Having returned to Lucille and family life, he finds that he, who defiantly in his youth "ain't studying *nobody,*" has raised this analytic intellectual, this detached and superior being. But the image is not punitive, as it registers, after all, his considerable achievement. Joe, himself, unlike his own father who abandoned him, has been a parent with a parent's pleasures and pains.

In the penultimate poem, "Easter Sunday, 1940," Lucille, attending church, has all the authority of a mother of a fine family:

> *A purity*
> *in sacrifice, a blessedness*
> *in shame.* Lucille
> in full regalia, clustered
> violets and crucifix.
> She shoos
> a hornet
> back to Purgatory,
> rounds the corner, finds
> her son in shirtsleeves staring

The cross-shaped stanza registering her splendor is a comic tribute to the majesty of her ascension. (The fact of Joe's return is given casually in the next stanza in parentheses; men are, after all, peripheral to the matriarchal household.) However, middle-aged Lucille in full religious glory is not complete without the voluptuous underlayer, the memory, in the final stanza of "Easter Sunday, 1940," of the "blushing thicket" in which her son was conceived.

The imagery of *Cameos,* sensual and religious, becomes ultimately cultural in tracing the survival of this family through the Depression years and into sight of the Promised Land, the American dream. The journey seems miraculous in every way. Yet in the final poem, "Nightwatch. The Son," the extreme right-hand justification of the stanzas signals the son's remoteness, in his astronomical study, from the varied visual patterns of family interactions that have characterized the nine preceding poems. The imagery is appropriate also for the poet's task as distant "witness" of this early-twentieth-century family who nevertheless "keep their / lives." Again, the ambiguity of "keep" finely registers both their integrity and the writer's recording intent. *Cameos* identifies what it takes for an African American family of Joe and Lucille's generation to produce a scientist son (as did Dove's own family in her father). It was to take another generation for the Dove family to produce a poet daughter.

Freedom: Bird's Eye View

Freedom: Bird's Eye View, the title of the second section of *On the Bus with Rosa Parks,* reflects, in part, an overview of the African American role in the nation's history but can also, I believe, be linked to the increasingly prominent public role that Dove had assumed in the nineties. *The Poet's World* (1995) is an expression of her role as poet laureate and poetry consultant to the Library of Congress (1993–95). It comprises the poem "Lady Freedom among Us" (discussed later in this chapter) and two lectures given during the period of her laureateship, "Stepping Out: The Poet in the World," and "A Handful of Inwardness: The World in the Poet." An essay titled "Autobiography" completes the collection. The frontispiece to *The Poet's World* is a photograph that shows Dove on the balcony outside the Poetry

Office at the Library of Congress. Dove herself commented on this view:

> The Poetry Office at the Library of Congress is tucked in a corner of what is called the "attic" of the Jefferson Building; someone once commented that the location was an indication of how the nation regards its artists, but I walk out on the balcony that looks over the Capitol, the Washington Monument, the Smithsonian and even the Jefferson Memorial on a clear day and think: "best view in town."[4]

Dove undoubtedly took the opportunity during her period at the Poetry Office to take an overview of the state of poetry in the nation and to think about the opportunities to promote literature more widely. She undertook a punishing schedule of engagements in school, colleges, libraries, and other public places to bring poetry alive for young people, almost to the point of endangering her own creativity. Some of the poems in this section are the fruit of that preoccupation with education, with the desire to communicate more widely and to reach out to the young. This kind of bird's eye view contrasts with that of "Ars Poetica" in *Grace Notes,* which had been, in part, a feminist rebuke to masculine literary egotisms. In "Ars Poetica," exasperated with the patriarchal stake out of the ground, Dove had declared, "Pencil me in as a hawk," choosing the aerial over the territorial as an image of artistic freedom. *Freedom: Bird's Eye View* similarly adopts the aerial, but it also signals a more hard-headed political, indeed, didactic, preoccupation with upbringing and education, as in "The First Book" and "Maple Valley Branch Library, 1967." In such poems, Dove overlooks the artistic health of the nation.

Cultural ideologies are under scrutiny in this section of the volume: the bird's eye view is, in part, an inspection of American values as they impact the young. The family is not always presented as a locus of security; children refract values in distorted and dangerous ways. The girl-child speaker of the poem "I Cut My Finger Once on Purpose," internalizing the family cult of masculine bravado, watches as her father "smashed a thumb in the Ford, / then stuck it in his mouth for show" and, duly hardened, responds to her brother being bought a "just-for-boys train" by braining him with the caboose:

>   he toppled
> from his rocker without a bleat;
> he didn't even bleed.

The poem is about the savagery of sibling rivalry and the child's confused response to being expected to grow up, put away childish toys, and to give way to another baby. She cultivates a festering malevolent regression, a bullying trepidation. Pitiful, she is not likeable. Family life in this scenario seems a breeding ground for monsters.

There is something of the rueful Prospero in Dove's acknowledgment of this "thing of darkness,"[5] this feminine Caliban in the cupboard, that is the dark side of the aerial spirit that lightens other poems in the section. The lighter note is at play in the poem "Freedom: Bird's-Eye View," which fantasizes soaring above the massed institutions of justice. The poem on the facing page, "Testimonial," revels in prelinguistic sensations and ironically acknowledges in the title that once words are attached to sensations, they have the formality and absurdity of a testimonial: sensory delight no longer leaks and melts but congeals into the platitude of "count my blessings." Language comes to stale and to set in order. Perhaps the poet is magically exempt in the concluding poem of the section, "Dawn Revisited," being given the "second chance," the "blank page," the "prodigal smell of biscuits." In imagination the poet has the freedom to begin again.

Culture and Nature

The title poem of the third section, *Black on a Saturday Night,* and "Singsong" (with a different title, "Song") from the second section, are taken from *Seven for Luck,* a song cycle for soprano and orchestra with lyrics by Rita Dove and music by John Williams.[6] "Black on a Saturday Night," evoking a specific ethnic and cultural energy, stands comparison with "Nigger Song: An Odyssey" from *The Yellow House on the Corner.* Whereas "Nigger Song" was an exercise in empathy, imitating the rush of energy of black youths, "Black on a Saturday Night" is both participative and ironically analytic in expression. Black is bold: Saturday night energy celebrates the moment, yet the poem plays with ideas, invoking and reversing conventional morality. The play on the word "attitude" is part of this word game. "Attitude" is a style statement, often a black style statement, but it is also self-perception, as in "an attitude will get you / nowhere fast." Attitude also signifies the perception of cultural groups by other cultural groups: "why are / you people acting this way." Pulsing against these ideas or abstractions about people (of which "black" is one) are the verbs "can" and "does," active and embracing: "black as black can." The repetitions, the swing, the turns of phrase are held, extended with humor, so that "tomorrow gives up with a shout."

The following two poems, "The Musician Talks about 'Process'" and "Sunday," are contrasting narratives of black masculine life-styles in the rural South. The first poem is subtitled "(*after Anthony 'Spoons' Pough*)," a tribute to the empathy between his blind musician grandfather and the animals that would listen to him playing the spoons. Like Orpheus with his lyre, he charmed nature. It is a nostalgic vision of one of the happier pastoral affinities of the old South. "Sunday," however, is about a "hunting man" whose savagery in providing for his family, trapping and gutting with "grim fury," is a twisted displacement of his own "animal" pain, which is also vented in strapping his children: "They were eating his misery / like bad medicine." Sunday, a day of leisure and leisure pursuits, is for this father a ferocious inverted reworking of old hatreds, internalized and self-destructive. Slaves would risk being beaten to death to escape to freedom; lynchings and beatings are the racist infrastructure of the South, but this man beats and leaves behind the "flesh and blood" of his own flesh and blood (the common term for "family") in his frantic assertion of manhood. "Sunday" is a sobering poem in which the Easter rabbit, caught and gutted, becomes a stark memorial of the blood and guts drained out in human sacrifice.

The poem that follows, "The Camel Comes to Us from the Barbarians," is close to "Sunday" in both theme and its readiness to transpose cultural binaries, the oppositions that create meaning and value, but it is expressed with humor. The most significant oppositions *within* a culture are those that culture creates in order to separate culture and nature. Nature is differentiated from culture but it is also assimilated, acknowledged, used by culture. The poem opens with the perspective of a barbarian (a cultural term that is immediately suggestive in a number of ways, including the idea of unrefined nature) faced, for the first time, with that strange phenomenon of nature, a camel:

> Hindquarters splayed, it tugs against its ropes,
> snorts, yearns its massive head and slavers
>
> toward that godawful sound.

Horrified by the camelness of the camel, the barbarian nevertheless assesses its commodity value; he adduces its serviceability. To seek to domesticate and reduce to servitude that which seems so alien is, by implication, as absurd as the idea of enslaving humans: both are inimical to the "sun-baked marketplace." The camel is scrutinized in the same way as early slave traders eyed up the humans they sold and regarded as barbarians. The ambiguity of the word "slavers" and the applicability of the word "monsters" to camels or to classes of humans, deepen the paradoxes of the poem.

The camel resists enslavement, but the "barbarians" are laying down the lines of civilization, trading and building (in the process enslaving animals and humans). Ironically, culture brings aesthetic and emotional refinement—costly commodities, as the closing lines of the poem indicate:

> A rare commodity, these beasts—
>
> who cannot know
> what beauty wreaks, what mountains
> pity moves.

The wit of the poem lies in the mordant evocation of gross nature under the appraising eye of "gross" culture. Camels seem so absolutely unmalleable as material, so crude and "rough cut," but the human eye, although appalled, is already shaping the creatures to human purpose considering the "measure of their service."

The above group of poems, "The Musician Talks about 'Process,'" "Sunday," and "The Camel Comes to Us from the Barbarians," explores the borders between human and animal existence, their affinities, relationships, and ways of naming. Used here about camels, words such as "creatures" and "beasts" have been used with derogatory cultural intent about humans, and "barbarians" is geographically descriptive but also means as if in a state of nature, raw and unrefined. Nature is always subject to cultural mediation: "The Camel Comes to Us *from* the Barbarians" [emphasis added].

The permutations of culture and nature are wittily reprised in the poem "The Venus of Willendorf," in which the poet visits the place where this legendary sculpture was unearthed. The comedy derives from Dove's amused realization that she herself, "a live black girl" is as much of a source of erotic wonder to the village community as had been the unearthing of the "sprawling buttocks and barbarous thighs" of the primitive Venus. The naive barbarism of the stares of contemporary provincial Austrians is an endurance test for the poet. She almost literally feels herself to be culturally constructed, "primitivized" by them as a contemporary black Venus of Willendorf. This experience has to be somehow ideologically aligned to the other characteristics of Austro-German culture, the high scholarship and the technological efficiency of the transport system. The wordplay of the poem bounces cheekily from culture to nature with a zest in verbal displacement, as when the innkeeper, beguiled by the "exotic" presence of "a live black girl," comments on the statue:

> Just a replica, *natürlich,*
> a handful of primitive stone

The unwitting erotic displacements implicit in words such as "handful" accrue to the point that the poet feels her own body "settle" into the image of the statue, experiences the "ripening / predicament of hip and thigh" as she is molded by the lascivious gaze of the local populace.

Lust overtakes both high and low in this bucolic setting. Invited to *"Herr Professor*'s summer house" for further elucidations of the mystery of that other Venus, the poet discovers that her presence moves him to confide that his pubic hair has gone white. Meanwhile, his wife, "hair too long and charred eyes / wild in their sockets . . . cleared away the tea things." As a narrative vignette of the intrusions of lust into polite society, this is exquisite social comedy, yet it is also a transforming moment of understanding how the intensity of a "gaze" might translate into the "visible caress" of a sculptor's hand. Just as the woman poet, amused, annoyed, or whatever, is nevertheless erotically aroused by the heat of the gaze, so art is envisaged as a visual climaxing between the physical body and the hand of the sculptor:

> what made
> the Venus beautiful
> was how the carver's hand had loved her,
> that visible caress.

The Venus of Willendorf is thus the expression of the artist's individual compulsive intensity, yet like any work of art, it also encompasses a broader cultural way of looking. This, too, has its comic analogy in the poem: the clumsy, communal, cumulative gawping of the modern day inhabitants of Willendorf shapes "a live black girl." Their very unrefinement is like a stamp of authenticity, a *natural* provenance for art.

If art is comically, intensely nature, it is also that accession to a heightened sensibility that draws on, is stimulated by, and lends enchantment to these collisions of the earth and social ritual. The statue known as the Venus of Willendorf is of the earth, earthy, but also, historically, the mark of a high cultural moment, a sign of a culture defining itself in a new way. The statue waited long in the earth for the miracle of rediscovery in a landscape now transformed by the modern miracle of express trains. The magic of the artist's gaze transforms the scene in the final stanza of the poem. The ameliorations, the harmonies of art, are graciously conferred upon technology in the vision of the express train (which earlier in the poem "barreled through" with ostentatious efficiency) now, in the evening,

> Lightning
> then a faint, agreeable thunder
> as the express glides past below,
> passengers snared in light, smudged flecks
> floating in a string of golden cells.

It is as if the artistic eye gives mystery to what is technological, banal, and familiar, just as the poem has earlier revealed the comic absurdities of daytime lust unexpectedly transformed into moments of erotic intimacy. This potency, this "rising hush," is akin to the potency of the long centuries during which the Venus lay hidden, untouched, unseen, unkindled. The complexity of the poem stems from its power to evoke such magical transformations from a platform of comedy. Dove bestows a benign pastoral haze upon midsummer antics.

Yet the idea of order that art renders has, at Willendorf, in the evening light, a more brutal sense of Pan's intolerable mysteries and absurdities than at Key West. Dove's poem registers a landscape of insight and blindness in which night drops "into the treeline like an ax," not the hauntingly distanced "ghostlier demarcations, keener sounds"[7] of Wallace Stevens's world of art in his poem "The Idea of Order at Key West." "*If only we were ghosts*" thinks the speaker of Dove's poem, still in the physical human dilemma, sexual and social, not abandoning it but willing, *natüralich,* to take the rough with the smooth.

It is characteristic of Dove's urbanity that this third section is not titled "The Pain of Being Black,"[8] although a number of the poems are about racist assumptions, racial disadvantage, and racial stereotypes. Dove always has time for the individual in his or her irrepressible presence. "Incarnation in Phoenix," a poem ostensibly about the difficulty of expressing breast milk after birth, has such a character in the "charcoal" midwife, an "African Valkyrie," who takes charge, "hair boiling / thunder over [a] rampart of bobby pins." The incarnation of the poem is not only the poet's new baby of mixed race but also the eruptive efficiency of the crisply white-clad nurse of African American–Norwegian parentage who impinges upon the scene to sort things out like an "envelope issuing smoke." Named Raven, she is the bringer of food in the desert and the phoenix from whose "smoke" the young phoenix can arise. The perspective of the poem is thus mythically witty, outward looking, and celebratory rather than in-turned and self-regarding. The same upbeat mode of recognition is evident in "My Mother Enters the Work Force," in which "the path to ABC Business School" is paid for by working as a seamstress. The imagery here, again feminine and feminist, harmonizes culture and nature in a zestful rendering of this journey of self-development. The achievements of ordinary African American women are celebrated further in the civil rights poems later in the volume.

Revenant

Revenant, the title of the fourth section of the volume, expresses the haunting quality of a number of poems not only within this section but also intermittently throughout the volume. A revenant is one who comes back from the dead, a ghost returning to haunt a significant location. The sense of return is, at times, personal memory in autobiographical poems recalling trivial irritations of spirit, but there is also a wider mandate, a reach that is historical and cultural.

The poems of larger scale enact a ritualized theater of collective failure. Most somber in this respect is "Revenant," the title poem of the section, in three stanzas, each with a final line dropped two lines below. How might the world be perceived by a returning spirit free to roam across centuries? The opening images of the first stanza are of natural majesty and freedom, although not without the shadow of cultural sway and rule. "Palomino," from the Latin *palumbinus,* is a horse resembling a dove (a play on the poet's own name) and associated with Native American Indians yet also with the imperialist Alexander the Great. The "gyrfalcon" is the Yeatsian symbol of cultural cycles, yet it inscribes an orbit beyond the naked eye, flies beyond the pale:

> Palomino, horse of shadows.
> Pale of the gyrfalcon
> streaking free,

a reckoning—

the dark climbing out a crack in the earth.

The term "pale" historically signifies the bounds of jurisdiction, and the expression "beyond the pale" is ambiguous in suggesting both physical escape from those bounds (the falcon's flight) and having gone beyond the moral limits prescribed by jurisdiction, that is, having become subject to "State" punishment. The opening stanza, then, for all the boldness of "streaking free," has already created linguistic tensions between liberty and law. It ends with the phrase "a reckoning" followed by the single dropped line that offers a deeply ambiguous image: "the dark climbing out a crack in the earth." The religious resonance of Christ's suffering and resurrection signal "dark" as being those whom society has collectively scapegoated, yet there is also, strangely, the opposite sense of the purposeful action of primal evil. Culturally, "pale" is the color of authority and boundary setting, so that, as in Dove's play *The Darker Face of the Earth,* there are further meanings: "the dark" can also represent the stigmatized "other" and the stain of evils such as slavery.

Darkness is associated with the state in the second stanza. For the rituals of punishment, figures of justice assume black and cover the face of the condemned with a black hood. The returning spirit might find the rituals of punishment different in kind on this stage: execution is a variant on crucifixion. The dropped single line of the second stanza is tersely diagnostic: "Gauze bandages over the wounds of State." This is what an execution (state or terrorist) amounts to, for all its deadly ceremony. It is a futile attempt on the part of society to staunch and cover its own failures. The visual transformation of the image from the black hood to the white bandage changes the concept from externally imposed justice to collective stigmata. Whatever color symbolism society invokes, it is immaterial to the victim "reeking with slobber" whose final sensation is of "no color."

That culture is intent upon visual display, as if in readiness to be pictorially recorded, is underlined in the third stanza:

> The canvas is primed, the morning
> bitten off but too much to chew.
> No angels here:
> The last one slipped the room
> while your head was turned,
>
> made off for the winter streets.

These lines give a bleak answer to the Rilkean question, "Who if I cried, would hear me among the angelic orders?"[9] In Dove's scenario, the enactment of state justice is no place for intermediaries of the spirit. The last angel has "slipped the room," or the *Raum,* the space that, as Rilke so hauntingly suggested, the human imagination always kept for unicorns or similar creatures of the spirit.[10] That the spirit of freedom is elusive and fugitive is ironically suggested in the colloquial language of the final line, in which the escaping angel "made off for the winter streets" unnoticed by the human spectator whose head "was turned" to the spectacle of execution that engrosses the center of the poem. The Rilkean angel is a being who acts as a kind of monitor of human progress. He is the invisible spirit measuring whether humans clinging to the visible have the potential to transform themselves spiritually into the invisible. In the angel the process is completed. A source of rebuke, terror, yet inspiration in Rilke's poetry, the angel is the spectator of our human imperfection, our adherence to the visible. In Dove's poem, the angel finds the visible in full sway; there is nothing to stay for.

The formal and rhetorical progression of "Revenant" is a movement from romantic symbolism in the images of natural freedom and range in the opening stanza to the neoclassic high-art freeze-frame and claustrophobic rigor of state authority and process in the middle stanza. It is as true of the images of freedom as it is of those of law that they inevitably carry some ideological taint, some color of assertion of rule. The rhetorical authority of these images, already exposed in the austere salience of the first two stanzas, is undermined by the colloquialism of the third. Elevation collapses into the clichéd phrase "bitten off but too much to chew." There is a shadow of a pun here in relation to the beheading, but most notably it draws attention to the inability of the human spirit to stomach what humans collectively do. While you, the human spectator, "turned" your head (to look toward or to look away, a privilege that "you" have as you are not having your head axed), angels "slipped the room." The "last one" "made off" out of the picture as if in Rilkean flight from the spectacle of humanity.

Dove has spoken of Wallace Stevens's idea of the poet as the "priest of the invisible" and her admiration for poets who try to express the inexpressible:

> Being articulate is not the key. You might have a prodigious command of language, but it's what happens between the words that matters; so much happens in the leaps, the silences. Its something I'm still wrestling with; I'm endlessly fascinated by it.

Dove goes on to say that she admires poems "in which the mundane and profound exist side by side, [in which] the cumulative effect is that the ineffable has been given a shape. Rilke addresses the ineffable all the time. . . . The unspoken assumption is that there exists something above words, beyond words that no language can touch."[11] "Revenant" is a major poem, "the mundane and the profound" linked in a feat of imagistic compression, yet this does not fully account for its effect. The pain of human history seeps through the lines like the blood of "wounds" whose color is omitted from the restricted palette of the poem. To claim the "ineffable" is a large claim, and Dove had no thought of making it for herself. The poem is a winter journey of the spirit, one in which the visible is unbearable and the invisible is, of course, always just missed, but it is also permeated with a Rilkean yearning that somehow the connectedness of the two might be discerned. If you could see an angel, you might be able to express the "ineffable," that which cannot be expressed.

The staging of the visible in the second stanza of "Revenant" is a "reckoning," a cost, from which the soul, like the angel, might do well to exit. The question of the soul's representation in the visible world preoccupies Dove in the *Revenant* section of this volume, as it was notably John Ashbery's theme in "Self-Portrait in a Convex Mirror," his meditation upon the self-portrait of sixteenth-century painter Parmigianino. Dove's poem "On Veronica" develops ideas of painting as a kind of shroud, or even a sloughed skin of the spirit that is reinvested with physicality. The glassy remoteness of the mirror in Ashbery's poem is replaced by a messier corporeality in Dove's artifacts.

The epigraph to Dove's poem is a description by painter Ewa Kuryluk of how she copied her own features onto a plastic sheet draped over a mirror, and the title, "On Veronica," draws a parallel with the story associated with St. Veronica. The saint, moved by the suffering of Jesus on his way to Calvary, is said to have wiped his face with a cloth on which his features then left an image. There seems to be a further reference in the poem to another kind of image taking—to the way photography captures a face, which is then followed by the developing process that gradually releases the features on to the negative. The name Veronica derives from "true image" (*vera icon*), perhaps also associated with the word "vernicle" for her veil or cloth, although there is no reliable evidence for the authenticity of the cloth (now in St. Peter's in Rome) or for her action. The paradox of the *veil* (the element at one remove), whether shroud, canvas, plastic sheet, or photographic plate, also being the *true* image, the element at one remove expressing physicality, is explored in the poem. These artifacts are the ghosts of the living beings, the "miraculous" traces from which we detect life. Materiality and spirituality are strangely commingled. Paint, in flagrant disregard of *noli me tangere* (the resurrected Christ's injunction not to touch him), is a painful, ecstatic resurrection:

> a wound. Skin talking:
> *yes there, touch me there.*
> The stain of a glance,

Painting and poetry, ekphrasis,[12] the verbal representation of visual representation, are also *involved* here, as in the first stanza of the poem in which the marks on the shroud / painting are "inscription." One medium is expressed in the veil of the other. "On Veronica" works harder for its effects than "Revenant." It might be called a flawed poem in relation to the perfection of the latter (which has the imagistic power of Plath's late *Ariel* poems). Yet there is something oddly appropriate about the imperfections of "On Veronica." The fascination with the physical erotic process of painting, its tangibility, recognizes the lack of this physical presence in writing. *Ut pictura poesis* (popularly, if inaccurately, translated "as in painting so in poetry") is not so easy a transition. One might also say that the gap between the painted canvas and what it purports to represent might be even larger, except that the canvas has its own self-authenticating physical existence, the "stain" of presence. The visible might or might not be the sign of the invisible, as Veronica's cloth might not bear the imprint of Christ's suffering features, but "On Veronica" gives more credence to the power of the visible than "Revenant." The visible might be an intersection of belief and disbelief, difficult to disentangle its truth or untruth as representation, yet the visible marks, in all their factitiousness, themselves solicit interpretation. It is as if they bring interpretation to bear.

The painter's power to interpret is the subject of "There Came a Soul," another poem about painting, but one that is more confident of poetry's power to add narrative to the relationship of painter and sitter. Ivan Albright's 1929 portrait of the twenty-year-old Ida Rogers, titled "Into the World There Came a Soul Called Ida," depicts her as an old woman. Dove's note to the poem informs the reader that art historians surmise that Albright's experience as a medical illustrator in the First World War might have been a predisposing factor in his later preoccupation with old age. Albright paints a young girl as an old woman, but Dove, as a poet, can represent how she must have actually looked, as well as the thought processes of the painter as he positioned his model, and the evolution of the canvas into a representation of old age. The painter interprets, but the poet can move around the interpretive process, has the edge in portraying memory, shifts of mood and perspective as an evolving interplay. The poem is complementary to "On Veronica": faking is a different kind of issue in a narrative imagining the thought processes of a painter. Whereas the shroud of a canvas is both conspicuously evidential as posthumous mark and encrypted with misrepresentation, Dove's verbal narrative acknowledges its own fictionality and moves easily between fact and imagining, ready to find inspiration in the interpretation or information provided by art historians. Verbal representation has the advantage of a temporal mobility of perspective.

Thus "There Came a Soul" opens by taking the story back (a version of *revenant*) to the arrival of Ida in the studio. She is not quite as she looks, the virginal appearance an illusion in this twenty-year-old wife and mother, the "gold band, the photographs" telling a different story than her appearance. The painter's slight disappointment, "He had hoped for a little more edge," gives way to his decisive placing of her. The transformational process in his visualizing of his model begins by placing her in an old chair. This active staging involuntarily releases wartime memories: the wicker chair was the one that had been some kind of solace amid the horrors of his occupation. The job of medical illustrator had been to "sketch / each clean curve of tissue opening," to keep a steady hand and eye while "wounded, swaddled shapes . . . moaned" and ether assailed his senses.

Albright expresses in the portrait all that he had to contain and edit out of the precision and objectivity of his wartime drawings. The portrait of Ida becomes a kind of self-portrait; the transference of image to canvas is a psychic transference, as, revenant, he returns the scene before him to the past, "applying paint / like a bandage to the open wound":

> until she was seated
> as he had been, dropped
> bleak and thick,
> onto the last chair in the world.

As the first stanza of the poem reminds us, Ida had come "solely at his bidding" in answer to his advertisement, and his portrait of her is the extreme of that painter's prerogative to subsume the sitter to the life of the painting. The incongruity of the title of the painting, "Into the World There Came a Soul Called Ida," emphasizes Albright's labor. It was, after all, Albright's experience that consisted of the "Pains and troubles" that Keats said were necessary "to school an Intelligence and make it a soul."[13] The painting's title also emphasizes *arrival,* as Dove's poem highlights. Like a visitant from another world of normality, "Pretty Ida, out to earn a penny / for her tiny brood," in Dove's narrative insertion is the precipitant of the painting, and she goes away afterward, having politely refused coffee. An autonomous spirit, she is only temporarily annexed. As the poem makes clear, she has another life. The painting itself has been given physical "birth" (a process cumbersome, like its title) because past and present "came" together.

Manifestations of spirit, both contemporary and in the form of ghostly visitants from the past, are brought into conjunction in a number of poems in the *Revenant* section. "*Götterdämmerung*" (Twilight of the Gods) and "Ghost Walk" seem such a pairing. Dove, in introducing "*Götterdämmerung*" at a reading in London,[14] said that the persona of the poem is the kind of elderly lady she had noticed walking a shopping mall for exercise before it opens. Even though the old lady knows she is "like some ancient / iron-clawed griffin," she has not stopped wanting to "sing Tosca or screw / James Dean." The celebration of this grit and determination, one kind of spirit, is countered by "Ghost Walk," which centers on the legend of a ghost haunting a Swiss chateau, a wife who, after her husband's death, remains enveloped in their love. The enjambment of the poem (there is no punctuation) and the present participles that extend through the eight octets express the continuity of the love. The hint of blues phrasing, the fairy tale elements, mythologize the paradoxes of an erotic odyssey so intense and exclusive. It seems appropriate that a life so given to memory should have an afterlife: the dead lady haunts the castle as if in search of the intensity of her living memories.

The *Revenant* section of *On the Bus with Rosa Parks* comprises a series of disturbing meditations on the soul's intensities and sicknesses, both individual and cultural. To return to the past or to visit again the spectacle of human degradation are occasions from which, like the angel in the poem "Revenant," the human desire is for escape. The two closing poems of the section, one public and exhortatory and the other more personal and private, look forward.

"Lady Freedom among Us," one of Dove's finest polemical and populist poems, was read by the poet at a ceremony to commemorate the two hundredth anniversary of the U.S. Capitol and the restoration of the Statue of Freedom to the Capitol dome on October 23, 1993. The poem was originally produced in an illustrated fine press edition and made globally available on the Internet, so it has been available both in an exclusive and in a widely accessible format. As poet laureate from 1993 to

1995 (and thereafter), Dove has embraced opportunities to extend the audience for poetry, saying, "If the fact that I'm a black woman makes a grandmother take her granddaughter to a reading that's fine."[15] The return of the statue to its place at the center of government (and close by the laureate's office) was an occasion to focus attention on its significance.

Less famous than the Statue of Liberty, the Statue of Freedom has equally important national meanings in relation to civil rights. "Lady Freedom among Us," from its opening lines, challenges those who might pass by:

> don't lower your eyes
> or stare straight ahead to where
> you think you ought to be going

The old-fashioned clumsy look of the statue is something we might avoid just as we might a strange person the street, but the uncompromising yet cajoling tone enjoins us to look up, to notice, and to participate. The "Us" of the title that puns on U.S. and the biblical phrasing of *"even the least of you"* signify inclusion. The statue is tough, resilient, the "thick skin of this town." That the statue has an especial significance for ethnic minorities is evident in the title. "Lady Freedom" is black phrasing, reminiscent of Billie Holiday, and it positions freedom as central to American culture: "she's not going to budge" and, in a word like "Among," as a homely presence. The poem, for all its apparent simplicity, is artfully anaphoric in its repeated exhortations and the drawing of the "many" into the "one" or, as the poem ends, "us." It is a considerable feat to have written a public poem in a diction that is warm, colloquial, direct, and even tenderly domestic yet also serious and uplifting with no hint of strain or pomposity. It acts as a prelude to the poem cycle in honor of Rosa Parks that concludes the volume.

The final poem of the *Revenant* section, "For Sophie, Who'll Be in First Grade in the Year 2000," although personal in dedication, begins with acknowledgment of the damage that has been done to the environment in the twentieth century: "No bright toy / this world we've left you." The address is direct, as in "Lady Freedom among Us," but invokes blessings: "May you / sleep in sweet breath." Millennial thoughts, looking back, return, taking stock, and soul searching suffuse the *Revenant* poems. Indeed, biographically, vicissitudes in Dove's life such as illness and the destruction of her home by fire following a lightning strike in 1998 must have required reserves of spirit to overcome. There is a dark edge to *Revenant,* but the literal meaning of "revenant," to come again, is not lost. The poem for Sophie on the threshold of the twenty-first century turns from the century that has been too acquainted with ashes to the child as promise of renewal with tender intimacy: "dear Sophie, / littlest phoenix."

Traveling the Century

The title sequence of ten poems, *On the Bus with Rosa Parks,* concludes the volume. Eight of the poems affirm the historical significance of the ordinary black women whose resistance to segregation embodied the civil rights movement. On December 1, 1955, in Montgomery, Alabama, Rosa Parks sat down in the front of a bus in the section reserved for whites and refused to move to the back, standing-only section for blacks. This became the catalyst that focused black determination to act concertedly in pursuit of equality with whites. Rosa Parks was not th~

woman to break Alabama's transportation laws: Claudette Colvin and Mary Louise Smith had earlier in the same year refused to give up seats on city buses, but it was felt by civil rights activists that, as a steady, respectable woman, Parks was more able to withstand the media attention of a test case through the Alabama courts.

The title of the first poem of the sequence, "Sit Back, Relax," mimics the soothing remarks addressed to passengers by attendants at the beginning of journeys—inappropriate, of course, for those who had to stand. The ten-line poem is as if in the mind of Rosa Parks or someone like her, weary, thinking of what to cook for supper, sick at heart. The phrases are well-worn expressions, their depth of feeling engrained in commonness: "Sometimes a body / just plain grieves." The final line, italicized and dropped below the others, is a prayer for God's help, as Christ prayed at the onset of his trial: "*Stand by me in this, my hour—.*" The ordinary has become the extraordinary. In a campaign based on the right to *sit down,* the words of religious entreaty, "*Stand by me,*" are ironic, in the same way as Martin Luther King declared the paradox that those who sat down were standing up for freedom. The civil rights journey, long and hard, has need of and honors the steadfastness of much-used words.

The third poem, "Freedom Ride," rewinds the film reel of history back to the conditions of the segregated South. This is like retaking a bus journey fraught with tensions through the ideological terrain of the names and events that are yet to unreel, the assassinations of Jack and Bobby Kennedy, Malcolm X, and Martin Luther King:

> Dallas playing its mistake over and over
> until even that sad reel won't stay

stuck—there's still
Bobby and Malcolm and Memphis,
at every corner the same
scorched brick, darkened windows.

The final stanza makes it firmly a personal responsibility whether you "ride" the bus or sit at home, take part or opt out, but "where you sit is where you'll be / when the fire hits." The journey motif, in this and other poems, with its ongoing continuity of past history and individual present action, emphasizes that the impulse of the section and of the volume is not only commemorative and honorific but also an exhortation to communal progress.

Most of these poems are based in the ordinary locations of segregation, highlighting the difficulties of protest and the vulnerabilities of those who brought about change. "Climbing In" is a version of the Red Riding Hood folktale, with the wolf as both bus driver and bus, and in a broader sense, the institutional structure that is threatening rather than protective. To climb into a bus in a segregated state was always a fearful experience for black people. The experience of joining the ride to freedom risked the danger of being eaten by the wolf.

Dove prefaced her reading of "Claudette Colvin Goes to Work" by saying that the poem is imagined as being spoken by Claudette Colvin (the teenager who in March 1955 refused to give up her seat on a bus), who now, in the 1990s, works in a care facility for the elderly.[16] The epigraph to the poem is a quotation from a boycott flyer put out after Rosa Parks was arrested in December. The flyer connects the two cases, and that of Mary Louise Smith (without mentioning her name), and warns, "*This must be stopped.*" Older now, Claudette Colvin takes the bus to work for the night shift. Her job, emptying bedpans, contrasts with her youthful fieriness, but the two so different kinds of actions are both part of her life's dedication to doing what is needed. Colvin and Smith, the latter an unmarried mother at the time, are not as frequently mentioned in books about the civil rights movement as Parks. Indeed, Parks was chosen by the black community as a test case just because she was an icon of respectability. For Dove, however, these young women who returned to private life are also to be honored in that the very unpremeditated nature of their response was human. The poem about Smith, "The Enactment," voices the caution of black activists in deciding against taking up her case:

> Can't use no teenager, especially
> no poor black trash . . .
>
> It's gotta be a woman,
> someone of standing . . .

Colvin and Smith did not have connections and influence, but what they did mattered. Parks took the heat of the flash-bulbs, but they prepared the way. "The Enactment" ends with the declaration that "only then," after the coming together of all these forces, both spontaneous and organized, can Rosa "sit down in the seat / we have prepared for her." "We" includes the girls who acted first, the black community who took up Rosa's case and posterity assigning her an honored position.

"Rosa," the simplest of the poems about this group of black women, is gravely anaphoric in the chiming of the opening and last stanza: "How she sat there. . . . How she stood up." The note is of wonder rather than of interrogation, but it is not portentously exclamatory: the small actions have taken on the weight of symbolic significance, but the language has not removed them from ordinary living. The poem is plain statement and riddling discovery: "the time right inside a place / so wrong it was ready." Parks's essential human dignity has become known, "carved by a camera flash," a phrase that encapsulates both the immediacy and the monumentalizing effect of publicity.

The ordinary journeys these women took to or home from work, which have become personal odysseys, a passage from one condition to another, are in contrast to the poet's more hedonistic journey in "QE2. Transatlantic Crossing. Third Day." The expansiveness of the long lines, after the taut concision of "Rosa," attests calmly to comfort and pleasure. Ocean liners are not buses: "the hush of trod carpet" and "cocktail piano," are phrases evocative of the absurdly enjoyable ambience. Dove does not try to attach herself to the moral high ground of the women she honors. Parks and Colvin experienced the struggle to overcome segregation as part of the daily struggle in their own neighborhood, whereas the poet, "from this rose-colored armchair,"

> can only imagine
> what it's like to climb the steel stairs and sit down, to feel
> the weight of yourself sink into the moment of *going home*.

The marine metaphors wittily endorse that they "sink," whereas the poet "float[s] on the lap of existence." The poet, a much-traveled successor of the late nineties, is a lighter, less-anchored being: "Well, I'd go home if I knew where to get off."

The meditation on "*living* history" continues in the penultimate poem of the volume, "In the Lobby of the Warner Theatre,

Washington, D.C.," which anxiously assesses Parks's presence, seated in a wheelchair (although she is not named in the poem) at a film premiere. Unease about the commercial pressures attaching themselves to this dignified figure "cajoled" to attend by the movie director, unsettles the poet's response. She, like the director, has annexed this living symbol. The helpless yet regal figure of Rosa Parks is positioned at the foot of the "golden escalator" to bear the stares of those "Scrolling earthward." The ideologies of political protest and commercial success are queasily united in the "camera flash" of fame. The metonymies of the poem brilliantly evoke the glamor, the surface of success, in the "cavalcade of murmuring sequins."

This celebrity cavalcade, with its "gush and coo," *descends* to her in homage to fame. Even in these surroundings, Parks is endowed with the resonance of all that she carries with her from a different world of experience:

> She waited. She knew how to abide,
>
> to sit in cool contemplation of the expected.
> She had learned to travel a crowd

Surprisingly, the religious strength of "abide" is in alliance rather than at odds with the ability to withstand and to ride publicity, "to travel a crowd." The inversions and unexpected turns of the verbs of stasis and motion throughout the poem are indicative of the transformations of the usual that Parks expresses. The American dream of fame and fortune, sought by those gawping at her, hungry for "true inspiration," cannot diminish her integrity.

The language of "In the Lobby of the Warner Theatre, Washington, D.C." is, in Bakhtinian terms, doubly oriented both to the language of celebrity and to the language of historical "truth." The poet has to make ideological adjustments in order to come to terms with the spectacle of this pioneer of civil rights in such a glossy milieu. Ideas of historical integrity and celebrity are in negotiation in the poem. As "*living* history," Parks, by her presence, brings the language zones of history and publicity into tension. (This is complicated by the fact that she is history just because of the publicity that her case attracted in the fifties.) In the nineties, at the media event of a film premiere, "the history she made for us sitting there" is ambiguously poised in meaning between an encounter with a celebrity and a reminder of how her original act of sitting down made history. Does the later occasion cheapen the earlier? With a generosity of spirit, Parks seems to "delight" in being at the premiere. Bakhtin refers to a "freedom connected with the relativity of literary and language systems," the freedom of moving "from one linguistic system to another."[17] (Bakhtin was specifically discussing the use of narrators in fiction, but his point has a more general application.) In language terms, the mixing of discourses is emblematic of Parks's struggle for the freedom not to be confined to one kind of discourse but to be plural and cross cultural barriers.

The title of the concluding poem of the collection, "The Pond, Porch-View: Six P.M., Early Spring," recalls the exactitudes of Thoreau's *Walden,* but the poem itself makes no claims for the precisions of thought or memory. The affinity to *Walden* is in acknowledging the small, the low-key, the down-to-earth, in having a place to pause awhile. If it is a moment to come down from the overview of the process of history that has informed the preceding poems, it nevertheless accepts that we cannot individually or collectively pause in our momentum forward into the next century. This autobiographical poem acknowledges that, in the group of poems as a whole, the chance has been missed to "recapture childhood's backseat / universe." Like it or not, the bus takes us

> through unfamiliar neighborhoods—
> chair in recline, the view chopped square
> and dimming quick.

The acceleration of time, the diminishments associated with ageing, "recline" being uncomfortably close to decline, are in view here. The bus journey is significant not only for its political resonance but also for a gathering symbolism. In Elizabeth Bishop's poem "The Moose," a bus and its freight of gossipy passengers become emblematic of transience, the human journey westward.[18] For Dove, the bus is progress, vehicle of transit through the changing American "neighborhoods." Her sense of the landscape, like her central image, is communal. There is a personal voice here, intimate and sharing, that sticks close to and trusts ordinary commonplace speech just because it has been rubbed and worn, not afraid to use the phrase "*living history*" to find out its connections. It seems apt that the title of the collection comes from a coincidence of the personal and the historical. While the poet and her daughter, Aviva, were being transported by bus on a university campus during a conference in 1995, Aviva excitedly pointed out that Rosa Parks was on the same bus. The title phrase, *On the Bus with Rosa Parks*, is both ordinary and extraordinary. That such an incident could be, at once so everyday and so steeped in momentous cultural change is at the heart of these poems. In this, her sixth collection of poetry,[19] Rita Dove extends and deepens our historical understanding of what Americans have made of themselves in the latter half of the twentieth century as they journey into the twenty-first.

CHAPTER 8

Postscript

American Smooth

Dove, in notes prefacing her latest volume, wrote that "American Smooth" is a "form of ballroom dancing" in which "the partners are free to release each other" and dance individually, "thus permitting improvisation and individual expression."[1] Dance poems thread three of the five sections. Emily Nussbaum, reviewing the volume, wrote: "For Dove, dance is an implicit parallel to poetry. Each is an expression of grace within limits; each is an art weighted by history but malleable enough to form something utterly new."[2] In poems such as "Fox Trot Fridays" (the title taken from a Nat King Cole song), "Bolero," American Smooth," and "Rhumba," lineation is a syncopated expression of rhythm. "Fox-Trot Fridays" moves

Smooth

as Nat King Cole's
slow satin smile

In "Rhumba," the lines antiphonally express a partnership that is also a contrast: on the left-hand side of the page, the smooth directions of the dance, and on the right, in italics, the effort of execution. The two columns can be read vertically as separate poems or across the page as a partnership, a partnership at once effortful and polished:

> *lean back, look at me—*
> lock your knees,
> > *the straighter your legs*
> look straight up
> > *the easier to fall,*

In this collection, however, dance is not all posed profession-
alism. The poem "Samba Summer" is a memory of a family
picnic in which the "Broke-leg cakewalk" and "high-butt
shenanigans" of the "drunken uncles" were center stage.

The second section of the volume, *Not Welcome Here,*
focuses on players in dance-hall bands and their experiences
prior to and during the First World War. The title recalls the attitudes of the American military command to African American
soldiers during the war. They were segregated and not regarded
as trustworthy in combat until the French asked for the aid
of the African American 369th Infantry Regiment (composed
largely of New York volunteers), which fought with great distinction. The first American regiment to arrive in France, the
369th "had logged the longest time in continuous combat"[3] by
the end of the war. Just as Robert Lowell honored the black
regiment of the Civil War,[4] Dove honors the black soldiers of
the American Expeditionary Force who fought in Europe in the
First World War. The poems shuttle between America and
France, recapturing the feelings and memories of African Americans in their differing wartime situations. Music is the expression of their spirit, energizing and restorative in the face of
racism in their own culture and in the hardships and dangers of
a soldier's existence.

Not Welcome Here opens with "The Castle Walk." Its ballroom dancing motifs connect with yet modify the harmonies of

the title poem. It is expressed from the viewpoint of the band-leader, James Rees Europe, who worked for the dance team, Vernon and Irene Castle. Their brand of ballroom dancing was the rage with wealthy New Yorkers in the war years. As the bandleader watches the "white folks stalk / through privilege," he thinks of how "Across the black Atlantic, / they're tram-pling up the map" of Europe. Whereas in "American Smooth" the dancer is involved in the ecstasies and agonies of creating flight and return, the tightly "gloved and buttoned" white dancers of "The Castle Walk" with "chins poked out" are con-stipated pedestrians, deaf to ragtime rhythms. Nevertheless, the bandleader lays down the tracks, and the poem lays down the phrases in empathetic enjambment:

> pour on

>> the violins, insinuate
>> a little cello,
>> lay some grizzly piano

>> under that sweet jelly roll.

This was New York in 1915. "The Passage," the second poem in journal form, is based on the wartime Atlantic cross-ing of Cpl. Orval E. Peyton, a veteran with whom Dove talked in 1987. The poem title and the phrase "Black Atlantic" from "The Castle Walk" call up memories of the infamous Middle Passage, the transportation of slaves by ship from Africa to America in earlier centuries. Robert Hayden's poem "Middle Passage" (1962) evokes the "charnel stench" of the holds in which the slaves were confined during those infamous jour-neys, the "dark ships" moving like "Shuttles in the rocking loom of history."[5] Corporal Peyton in his Atlantic journey to

Europe in 1917 has the freedom to move about the ship, to come up for air when it is suffocating below in the unventilated quarters. Yet however unlike the wretched slaves of the transports, he is similarly in limbo, in passage between two continents and two lives. Enlistment, for a black American who had never been out of his home state, was an opportunity for education, training, for the stimulus of travel, for wartime camaraderie. Not that Americans were cheering encouragement to their black compatriots volunteering for service. There was no send off from Newport for the 372nd Infantry, only "a few colored people" to watch them go. Corporal Peyton's diary records the basic things that preoccupy the ordinary soldier, including seasickness, food, conditions, and the boredoms and tensions of the voyage, yet also how the high spirits of the men impress the hard-bitten sailors.

The following four poems express the responses of soldiers on the battlefields of France, including those who played in the famous 369th Infantry band led by James Rees Europe. In the poem "Noble Sissle's Horn," Noble Sissle (the drum major of the band), a famous jazz cornet player and entertainer, remembers the racist insult he endured while training in South Carolina.[6] The poem alternates italicized sections of these memories with his sense of expertise in horn playing:

> *(Take your hat off, boy.*
> *Not quick enough.*
> *Pick it up! Too slow.)*
>
> A horn needs to choke on
> what feeds it,

The control of technique has been tempered in his endurance of abuse. Yet Sissle feels that with nations mowing each other down, "a man can hoot just as well as holler." If Sissle represents nobility, the artistic spirit surviving adversity, "Alfonso Prepares to Go over the Top" is the last thoughts of a battle-hardened soldier before his death. Alfonzo anticipates his knife warming itself in the "gut of a Kraut." It is a "long corridor" from his childhood; there is no music in this poem. The subtitle, "(*Belleau Wood, 1917*)," locates the poem in one of the most dreadful and bloody arenas of warfare, with patches of land taken and retaken with horrific fatalities.[7]

In "La Chapelle. 92nd Division. Ted," the soldier, in the chill of autumn on the "bitter ridge" of France, remembers the "red earth" of Louisiana, yet he is not nostalgic. The "stunned lavenders and pinks / dusted with soot" that he glimpses by the roadside are, like himself, survivors. The Ninety-second Division was damaged by racist hostility from American higher command, badly equipped and poorly deployed without support,[8] yet Dove shows how the individual soldier, in spite of this, has his own moments of perception and restoration. "Variations on Reclamation," set in a hospital in Aix-le-Bains in 1918, follows the slow recovery of Teddy, a wounded soldier (possibly an amputee) pining because there is no music to raise his spirits. Ironically, his painful learning to walk again is the only "tap-step" to be heard. But his experience had almost destroyed his capacity for music:

> He'd been to the mountain
> and found it green and trembling
>
> with its fallen. He'd called out
> so many times to those lost last breaths

The religious echo here, "He'd been to the mountain," is faint, not visionary as in Martin Luther King's later famous speech in Memphis.[9] The return to America produces another variation on pain: a decorated war hero, Teddy is nevertheless the butt of racist jokes jeering at his disability: "*Boy, / we told you to watch your step.*"

The 369th was one of the few returning black regiments to be feted. In "The Return of Lieutenant James Reese Europe," the bandleader, playing French marches with his band in the Victory Parade in New York in February 1919, remembers their arrival in France in 1917 and the welcome given them by the French. He recalls how meanly the black infantry were equipped, yet as a band, they gave a thirty-seven-day concert trip throughout France, raising the spirits of troops and civilians. Now, in marching past the Flatiron Building, his thoughts are cynical about American attitudes to black soldiers:

> Miss Flatiron with your tall cool self: How do.
>
> You didn't want us when we left but we went.
> You didn't want us coming back but here we are,
> stepping right up white-faced Fifth Avenue in a phalanx[10]

Returning is returning to racism, and it is only when they see the "brown faces" of Lenox Avenue, are they really at home.

"Ripont," the final poem of *Not Welcome Here*, recalls the journey of the poet with her husband and baby daughter, Aviva, to the French village where in the September offensive of 1918, as the epigraph from *The Unknown Soldiers* records, the black soldiers fought bravely. The American family came by chance upon a memorial service for the fallen French and Negro soldiers:

> Everyone smiled at us sadly, they thought
> we were descendants too

> What else could we do we smiled back
> we let them believe

The experience was unsettling. Dove was unable to write anything about it and "wrote nothing / for thirteen years not a word in my notebook / until today," the day her daughter was *"leaving home,"* as if maternal pride and anxiety somehow brought that earlier experience to bear. Visiting Ripont placed the poet in a false light as a descendant of a fallen soldier: *then* there was no historical family connection. But at the point of writing, memory connects. The poem, in nine verse paragraphs, has no punctuation, no stops, although it does have capital letters where the stops would have been. The lack of punctuation accentuates time in a curious way. The poet records tracing the sites of loss and devastation while her young child happily crows and gurgles. The tensions set up by such a situation are expressed in the edginess of unpunctuated lines searching back yet also carrying forward and culminating, unexpectedly, in the dedication, *"for Aviva leaving home."* The poet makes no claim that this loss is in any way like the bereavements of war. Rather, the ordinary personal memory comes to represent the larger acts of community and memory. The merging of paths, when the American family followed the French cars driving away from the memorial service, is a fortuitous and benign parallel of the wartime fellowship of the French and the African American soldiers:

> we drove with the crowd
> single file through the woods to the river
> where we turned left they turned right
> some of them waving
> our daughter waving back

The poems of *Not Welcome Here* reveal Dove's historical consciousness bridging the past and the present (bridge, or "pont" in French, is in the name "Ripont"). One aspect of that bridge is implicit in the dedication to Aviva, of German and American parentage, a "descendant" of grandparents whose two countries were at war. This moving sequence of poems highlights the individual experiences and memories of the African American soldiers, honoring their achievements, just as the French honored them.

If dance bands and dancing are the musical thrum of *American Smooth,* it should be noted that the volume opens with "All Souls'," a poem about the expulsion from the Garden of Eden. The poem was part of Dove's struggle to write her way out of the sense of loss after the fire that destroyed her home in Charlottesville, Virginia, in 1998. Many of her manuscripts were destroyed. In "All Souls'," the "din" of animal and bird sounds fades as Adam and Eve encounter "silence" outside the gate. In time they fill the silence with "sighs," but with their

> heads tilted as if straining
> to make out the words to a song
> played long ago, in a foreign land.

Although Adam and Eve had spent time in Eden naming the creatures (who had their own signifying and expressive cries), they are at a loss now to articulate their own songs. The poem expresses a personal pain that is also a universal artistic fear of loss and disconnection with nature. In terms of language as definition or as emotional expression, "All Souls'" also connects with the sequence of pattern poems, "Twelve Chairs." These poems were carved on the backs of marble chairs in the lobby

of the Federal Court House in Sacramento, California.[11] Dove
said that the chairs were around a circular table and so could be
read in any order rather than in the sequence of the book. The
poems express the differing attitudes of randomly selected jurors.
In "First Juror," legalistic and natural imagery is at variance:

> Proof casts a shadow;
> doubt is to walk
> onto a field
> at high noon
> one tendril
> held to
> the
> wind.

Dove pointed out that the poems were placed centrally in the
third section of five because they were the "fulcrum" of a collection that "is all about our particular, American brand of justice."[12]

Much of the collection is about American injustices of the
past. The poem "Hattie McDaniel Arrives at the Coconut
Grove," in the fourth section titled *Blues in Half-Tones,
³/₄ Time,* is the most notable example in addition to the *Not
Welcome Here* sequence. Hattie McDaniel was the first African American to win an Oscar as best actress in a supporting
role for her role as Mammy in *Gone with the Wind.* When the
film premiered in Atlanta, a segregated city, in 1939, Hattie
was not invited, and her picture was taken off the back of the
movie program. However, she was able to attend the 1940
Academy Awards dinner in the Coconut Grove nightclub of the
Ambassador Hotel in Hollywood. The poem opens by capturing the fizz of her arrival:

> late, in aqua and ermine, gardenias
> scaling her left arm in a spasm of scent,
> her gloves white, her smile chastened, purse giddy
> with stars

As well as working as a singer and a bit part actress, Hattie McDaniel, in the early part of her career, had hired herself out as a maid when acting was hard to come by. Dove concocts, in the main body of the poem, an extravagant confection of Hattie's life, her marriages, roles, nicknames, sayings, her indomitable spirit, and the fact that she continued to accept stereotypical black roles as a domestic, "a truckload of aprons and headrags" (she preferred playing a domestic to being one). The poem celebrates her giddiest moment of fame. It doesn't mention her exclusion from the film premiere in Atlanta, but this kind of racist injustice, with which she had always contended, intensifies the significance of her arrival:

> It's a long beautiful walk
> into that flower-smothered standing ovation,
> so go on
> and make them wait.

Dove celebrates the personal triumph over injustice, the system having to give way to Hattie, "no corset wide enough / to hold you in."

The fifth and final section of the volume, *Evening Primrose*, highlights nature. This is perhaps surprising in a poet who has never been an avowed nature lover, who acknowledges, in "Reverie in Open Air," that she is "Out of sync with wasp and wren" and prefers "books to moonlight." Yet in the poem

"Evening Primrose," the flower, blazing at night, is implicitly an image not only of the writer's own secret labor (Dove likes to work at night) but also of deferral, the storing of experience to come into expression out of darkness, at a later time. The poem "Desk Dreams" recalls the poet's work rooms in different locations in which nature is variously soothing, like the cicada in Arizona, or intimidating, like the "chill Cyclopean blue" of Lake Como in Italy, or invigorating, like the blue sky overhead as the poet surveys her ruined desk after the fire that destroyed her house. In the final poem, "Looking Up from the Page, I Am Reminded of This Mortal Coil," the poet, after working at night, contemplates daybreak. This is color from the "heavenly paintshop" but also—as if to recall "All Souls'," the first poem of the collection, as well as the African American dance bands— music:

> The blaze freshens,
> five or six miniature birds
> strike up the band.

Dawn, the time to pack up writing, is a reminder that there will be a time when the "play's over," when we shuffle off this mortal coil, but it is also nature's renewal, a new day.

Notes

Chapter 1—Introduction

Some of the interviews with Dove originally published in journals or in collections of interviews with several writers that I have quoted in the notes have recently been collected in a book edited by Earl G. Ingersoll, *Conversations with Rita Dove* (Jackson: University Press of Mississippi, 2003). In these instances, I have given the journal reference (or other earlier reference) and, in parentheses, the Ingersoll collection page reference.

1. Malin Pereira, "Appendix: Interview with Rita Dove," *Rita Dove's Cosmopolitanism* (Urbana: University of Illinois Press, 2003), 166 (Ingersoll, *Conversations,* 154).

2. Ibid., 166 (Ingersoll, *Conversations,* 154).

Chapter 2—*The Yellow House on the Corner*

Quotations from poems in Rita Dove's *The Yellow House on the Corner* are from the 1980 edition (Pittsburgh: Carnegie Mellon University Press). Some of the interviews with Dove, first published in journals, have been collected in Ingersoll's *Conversations*. In these cases, I have given both the original journal reference and, in parentheses, the Ingersoll collection page reference.

1. Rita Dove, introduction to Rita Dove, *Rita Dove: Selected Poems* (New York: Vintage Books, 1993), xxi.

2. Ibid., xx.

3. Mohammed B. Taleb-Khyar, "An Interview with Maryse Condé and Rita Dove," *Callaloo* 14, no. 2 (1991): 345 (Ingersoll, *Conversations,* 77).

4. Ekaterini Georgoudaki, "Rita Dove: Crossing Boundaries," *Callaloo* 14, no. 2 (1991): 420.

5. Pereira, "Interview with Rita Dove," 173 (Ingersoll, *Conversations,* 159).

6. Helen Vendler, "Rita Dove: Identity Markers," in *The Given and the Made* (London: Faber, 1995), 68.

7. Wallace Stevens, *Collected Poems of Wallace Stevens* (London: Faber, 1955), 534.

8. Taleb-Khyar, "Interview with Maryse Condé and Rita Dove," 356 (Ingersoll, *Conversations*, 81).

9. Vendler, "Rita Dove," 63.

10. Ibid., 66.

11. Toni Morrison, "The Pain of Being Black," *Time*, May 22, 1989.

12. Stevens, *Collected Poems*, 534.

13. *Questions of Travel* is the title of Elizabeth Bishop's 1965 volume of poetry.

14. "To Marguerite," in *The Poems of Matthew Arnold*, ed. Kenneth Allott (London: Longmans, 1965), 124.

15. Vendler, "Rita Dove," 63.

Chapter 3—*Museum*

Quotations from the poems in Rita Dove's *Museum* are from the 1983 edition (Pittsburgh: Carnegie Mellon University Press).

1. The subtitle of this chapter is from the poem "Dusting" in Rita Dove, *Museum*, 9.

2. My reference is to the version published in Marianne Moore, *Complete Poems* (London: Faber, 1981), 32.

3. Stan Sanvel Rubin and Judith Kitchen, "'The Underside of the Story': A Conversation with Rita Dove," in *The Post-Confessionals: Conversations with American Poets of the Eighties*, ed. Earl G. Ingersoll, Judith Kitchen, and Stan Sanvel Rubin (London: Associated University Presses, 1989), 157 (Ingersoll, *Conversations*, 7).

4. William Walsh, "Isn't Reality Magic? An Interview with Rita Dove," *Kenyon Review* 11, no. 3 (Summer 1994): 149.

5. Christian Schad (1894–1982) was a painter of the Neue Sachlichkeit movement of German realism in the 1920s. *Sachlichkeit*

means "reality," "objectivity," "detachment." The movement was a reaction to the First World War, and it marked a determination to engage with the facts of real life, to bear witness to the realities of city life. The movement was expressed in Schad's paintings of this period by a series of portraits of uncompromising linearity in a dry, harshly lit space in which figures are uncomfortably fore-grounded. Dove refers to Schad's self-portrait of 1927 (in a green diaphanous silk shirt that unforgivingly reveals his hairy chest) in lines 13–16.

6. Dove first saw "Agosta the Winged Man and Rasha the Black Dove"(German title "Agosta, der Flügelmensch und Rasha, die Schwarze Taube") at the exhibition "Christian Schad," Staat-liche Kunsthalle, Berlin, June 28–August 24, 1980. She afterward met and talked to the artist on several occasions (information sup-plied by Dove). The portrait, oil on canvas, is currently (2005) in the Tate Modern, London, on loan from an anonymous private collector.

7. Walsh, "Isn't Reality Magic?" 151.

8. *Ut pictura poesis:* a phrase used by the Roman poet Horace in his essay *Art of Poetry*. Literally, it means "poetry is like painting" but has become famous in the inaccurate translation "as in painting, so in poetry."

9. *Ekphrasis:* originally, in the plural, *ekphrases,* the title of a series of essays vividly describing paintings by the Greek writer (one of a family of rhetoricians called Philostratus), now usually known as Philostratus IV, who lived in the first century B.C. See notes 11 and 12 below.

10. Walsh, "Isn't Reality Magic?" 51.

11. James Heffernan, *Museum of Words: The Poetics of Ekphra-sis from Homer to Ashbery* (Urbana: University of Chicago Press, 1993), 3.

12. Heffernan, *Museum of Words,* 6.

13. Rubin and Kitchen, "Underside of the Story," 157 (Ingersoll, *Conversations,* 7).

14. In Rubin and Kitchen, "Underside of the Story," Dove speaks of her awareness that Europeans saw her as representative, "'an object,' . . . they weren't seeing *me,* but a shell" (157) (Ingersoll, *Conversations,* 7).

15. Tom Brazaltis, "Poet in Motion," *Plain Dealer,* February 26, 1995, 14.

16. Rubin and Kitchen, "Underside of the Story," 158 (Ingersoll, *Conversations,* 8).

17. "The Emperor of Ice Cream" is the title of a poem by Wallace Stevens. See Stevens, *Collected Poems,* 64.

18. Sylvia Plath, *Sylvia Plath: Collected Poems,* ed. Ted Hughes (London: Faber, 1981), "The Colossus," 129; "Daddy," 222; "Ariel," 239.

19. Patricia Kirkpatrick, "The Throne of Blues: An Interview with Rita Dove," *Hungry Mind Review* 35 (1995): 36–37.

20. Therese Steffen, *Crossing Color: Transcultural Space and Place in Rita Dove's Poetry, Fiction, and Drama* (Oxford: Oxford University Press, 2001), 176.

21. Mikhail Bakhtin emphasized that the language of a novel is an interweaving of a number of cultural voices, a "heteroglossia." Thus fiction is inherently "dialogic," in dialogue with, and angled toward, the different speech communities (or language zones) that constitute culture. The narrator's discourse is not a single voice but imports and naturalizes the speech of others. Parodic stylization draws attention to the ideological assumptions and values of the different cultural zones. See Mikhail Bakhtin, "Discourse in the Novel," in *The Dialogic Imagination: Four Essays by M. M. Bakhtin,* trans. Caryl Emerson and Michael Holquist, ed. Michael Holquist (Austin: University of Texas Press, 1981), 259–63.

22. Rubin and Kitchen, "Underside of the Story," 155 (this section of the interview has been omitted from Ingersoll, *Conversations*).

23. Ibid., 154 (omitted from Ingersoll, *Conversations*).

24. Ibid., 156 (Ingersoll, *Conversations,* 6).

25. Ibid., 159 (Ingersoll, *Conversations,* 9).

Chapter 4—*Thomas and Beulah*

1. Steven Schneider, "Coming Home: An Interview with Rita Dove," *Iowa Review* 19, no. 3 (Fall 1989): 112 (Ingersoll, *Conversations*, 62).

2. See the catalogue (illustrated in color) to the touring exhibition of 1993–95, *Jacob Lawrence: The Migration Series*, ed. Elizabeth Hutton Turner (Washington, D.C.: Rappahannock Press and Phillips Collection, 1993). The quotation is from an essay in that catalogue by Lonnie G. Bunch III and Spencer R. Crewe, "A Historian's Eye: Jacob Lawrence, Historical Reality, and the *Migration* Series," 23.

3. Schneider, "Coming Home," 116 (Ingersoll, *Conversations*, 67).

4. Quoted in Jeffrey C. Stewart, "(Un)Locke(ing) Jacob Lawrence's Migration Series," in *Jacob Lawrence: The Migration Series*, ed. Elizabeth Hutton Turner (Washington, D.C.: Rappahannock Press and Phillips Collection, 1993), 45–46.

5. Steven Bellin, "A Conversation with Rita Dove," *Mississippi Review* 23 (1995): 28 (Ingersoll, *Conversations*, 132).

6. Schneider, "Coming Home," 116 (Ingersoll, *Conversations*, 66). Malin Pereira has noted that the photograph of the couple on the cover of the 1986 Carnegie Mellon University Press edition of *Thomas and Beulah* is not of Dove's grandparents but of an aunt and uncle from her father's side of the family. Malin Pereira, *Rita Dove's Cosmopolitanism* (Urbana: University of Illinois Press, 2003), 101 and 114n12.

7. Schneider, "Coming Home," 117 (Ingersoll, *Conversations*, 67).

8. Lynn Keller, "Sequences Testifying for 'Nobodies': Rita Dove's *Thomas and Beulah* and Brenda Maria Osbey's *Desperate Circumstance, Dangerous Woman*," in *Forms of Expansion: Recent Long Poems by Women* (Chicago: University of Chicago Press, 1997), 115. Keller quotes from Lawrence Levine, *Black Culture and Black Consciousness: Afro-American Folk Thought from Slavery to Freedom* (New York: Oxford University Press, 1977), 240.

9. Rita Dove in Rubin and Kitchen, "Underside of the Story," 161 (Ingersoll, *Conversations*, 10).

10. Quotations from *Thomas and Beulah* are from Dove, *Selected Poems*.

11. F. Scott Fitzgerald, *The Great Gatsby* (1926; reprint, Penguin, 1950), 187.

12. Robert McDowell, "The Assembling Vision of Rita Dove," in *Conversant Essays: Contemporary Poets on Poetry,* ed. James McCorkle (Detroit: Wayne State University Press, 1990), 300.

13. Fitzgerald, *Great Gatsby,* 188.

14. John Shoptaw, "Segregated Lives: Rita Dove's *Thomas and Beulah,*" in *Reading Black, Reading Feminist: A Critical Anthology,* ed. Henry Louis Gates Jr. (London: Penguin, 1990), 375.

15. John Shoptaw has noted the "synecdochal flourish" as a stylistic feature of the poem. Shoptaw, "Segregated Lives," 378.

16. Roland Barthes, *A Lover's Discourse,* trans. Richard Howard (New York: Hill and Wang, 1978), 2.

17. Ibid., 59.

18. Ibid., 2.

19. Rita Dove in Schneider, "Coming Home," 118 (Ingersoll, *Conversations,* 68).

20. Rita Dove said, "While I was writing this book I was playing a lot of music, everything from Lightnin' Hopkins to older ones like Larry Jackson or some of the recordings that Al Lomax made of musicians, all the way up to Billie Holiday, stopping about in the '50s. It seemed to be the music for the book." Schneider, "Coming Home," 118 (Ingersoll, *Conversations,* 68).

21. In this reading of Thomas's feelings as part of the ups and downs of married life, I differ from Shoptaw, who, in "Segregated Lives," emphasizes segregation as the characteristic governing their lives in all respects, including their marriage.

22. In Vendler, "Rita Dove," 79–82.

23. Rubin and Kitchen, "Underside of the Story," 156 (Ingersoll, *Conversations,* 6).

24. Rita Dove in Schneider, "Coming Home," 116 (Ingersoll, *Conversations,* 66).

25. Rita Dove in ibid., 119 (Ingersoll, *Conversations,* 69). Dove says in the interview that it was her grandmother who mentioned that her grandfather had dared his best friend to swim the river on the journey north, and that what intrigued her, as a writer, was his silence on the subject.

26. Ekaterini Georgoudaki emphasizes Beulah's "encaged" spirit in Georgoudaki, "Rita Dove," 428.

27. Emily Walker Cook has argued that "Beulah endured incestuous advances, if not outright rape, from her drunken father." "'But she won't set a foot / in his turtledove Nash': Gender Roles and Gender Symbolism in Rita Dove's *Thomas and Beulah,*" *College Language Association Journal* 38, no. 3 (March 1995): 324. My own view is that this is expressed as a possible danger rather than an actual case of abuse.

28. McDowell, in "Assembling Vision of Rita Dove," 301, reads this passage more severely as "men in collusion have delivered her up to her fate."

29. Ibid.

30. Published in Rita Dove, *Rita Dove: The Poet's World* (Washington, D.C.: Library of Congress, 1995). See page 15.

31. A phrase from the finale of George Eliot's *Middlemarch* (1871–72) (London: Penguin, 1965), 896, in which the narrator pays tribute to the "hidden life" of those like Dorothea who have not had the opportunity to live a more public, professional life.

32. John Murphy, "John Ashbery: An Interview," *Poetry Review* 75, no. 2 (August 1985): 25.

33. A phrase from "Lightnin's Boogie" by Lightnin' Hopkins.

34. "Dream Boogie," in Langston Hughes, *Selected Poems of Langston Hughes* (New York: Vintage Classics Edition, 1990), 221.

35. Part of the title of his essay cited in note 12 above.

36. Dove, introduction to *Selected Poems,* xxi.

37. From Tom Paulin, *The Strange Museum* (London: Faber, 1980), 11.

38. Rubin and Kitchen, "Underside of the Story," 162 (Ingersoll, *Conversations*, 10).

39. Quoted from Rainer Maria Rilke, *Rilke: Selected Poems*, trans. J. B. Leishman (London: Penguin, 1964), 35.

40. Quoted from Michael Hamburger, trans. and ed., *An Unofficial Rilke* (London: Anvil Press, 1981), 115.

41. Patricia Wallace, "Divided Loyalties: Literal and Literary in the Poetry of Lorna Dee Cervantes, Cathy Song, and Rita Dove," *Melus* 18 (Fall 1993): 12–13.

Chapter 5—*Grace Notes*

Quotations from poems in Rita Dove's *Grace Notes* are from the 1989 edition (New York: W. W. Norton).

1. Helen Vendler, "An Interview with Rita Dove," in *Reading Black, Reading Feminist*, ed. Henry Louis Gates Jr. (London: Penguin, 1990), 486.

2. From "Summit Beach, 1921."

3. Bonnie Costello, "Scars and Wings: Rita Dove's *Grace Notes*," *Callaloo* 14, no. 2 (1991): 434.

4. The titles of two poems by Walt Whitman, on 275 and 281 of *Walt Whitman: Collected Poems* (London: Penguin, 1975).

5. Wallace Stevens, "Credences of Summer," in Stevens, *Collected Poems*, 377.

6. Hughes, *Selected Poems*, 4. I am indebted to Therese Steffen for this reference (see Steffen, *Crossing Color*, 184–85n).

7. The three quotations are from Rainer Maria Rilke, *Duino Elegies*, trans. J. B. Leishman (London: Chatto and Windus, 1975), 37. "The Second Elegy" was written mainly in 1912.

8. "Shades of the prison-house begin to close / Upon the growing Boy." William Wordsworth, "Ode: Intimations of Immortality," in *Selected Poems*, ed. Walford Davies (London: Dent, 1975), 107.

9. Rilke, *Selected Poems,* 38.

10. Elizabeth Bishop, *Elizabeth Bishop: Complete Poems* (London: Chatto and Windus, 1991), 159.

11. *The Poetry of Robert Frost,* ed. Edward Connery Lathem (New York: Henry Holt, 1969), 377.

12. Walsh, "Isn't Reality Magic?" 150.

13. Steffen, *Crossing Color,* 4–5.

14. Plath, *Collected Poems,* 239.

15. Vendler, "Rita Dove," 85.

16. See Hélène Cixous, "The Laugh of the Medusa," trans. Keith Cohen and Paula Cohen, in *New French Feminisms,* ed. Elaine Marks and Isabelle de Courtivon (Brighton: Harvester Press, 1981).

17 .Vendler, "Rita Dove," 87.

18. *Keats: The Complete Poems,* ed. Miriam Allott (London: Longman, 1970), 541.

19. Bellin, "Conversation with Rita Dove," 20 (Ingersoll, *Conversations,* 127).

20. T. S. Eliot, *T. S. Eliot: Collected Poems* (London: Faber, 1963), 63.

21. Taleb-Khyar, "Interview with Maryse Condé and Rita Dove," 365 (Ingersoll, *Conversations,* 86).

22. Bellin, "Conversation with Rita Dove," 29 (Ingersoll, *Conversations,* 132).

23. "An Interview by Grace Cavalieri,"American Poetry Review 24 (March/April 1995): 15 (Ingersoll, *Conversations,* 143).

24. "Poetry, Politics and Intellectuals," in *The Cambridge History of American Literature,* ed. Sacvan Bercovitch (Cambridge: Cambridge University Press, 1996), 8:153–54.

25. Quoted from a letter to Charles Eliot Norton, February 4, 1872, in *Henry James: Letters,* ed. Leon Edel (London: Macmillan, 1974), 1:274.

26. Dove discusses "diaspora" in her conversation with Therese Steffen: "I believe that one of the most liberating revelations for this country would be to recognize that all of us are in a diaspora—not

just blacks or immigrants, but everyone of us. This nation is founded on the concept of diaspora." Steffen, *Crossing Color,* 171.

Chapter 6—*Mother Love*

Quotations from poems in Rita Dove's *Mother Love* are from the 1995 edition (New York: W. W. Norton). The chapter subtitle is from "Lamentations" on page 57.

1. Rita Dove, "An Intact World," foreword to Dove, *Mother Love,* xi.

2. Stephen Cushman, "And the Dove Returned," *Callaloo* 19, no. 1 (1996): 132.

3. A phrase from "Heroes," in Dove, *Mother Love,* 3.

4. Roland Barthes, "Writing and the Novel," quoted here from the translation by Annette Lavers and Colin Smith in *Writing Degree Zero* (New York: Hill and Lang, 1967), 30.

5. John Milton, *Paradise Lost,* ed. Alistair Fowler (London: Longmans, 1968), bk. 4, p. 210, ll. 268–72. Proserpine, Dis, and Ceres are other names for Persephone, Hades, and Demeter.

6. Rainer Maria Rilke, *Rainer Maria Rilke: Sonnets to Orpheus,* trans. C. F. MacIntyre (Berkeley and Los Angeles: University Press of California, 1960), 1.1, p. 3.

7. Stevens, *Collected Poems,* 76.

8. Rilke, *Sonnets to Orpheus* 2.14, p. 83.

9. Dove, "Intact World," xii.

10. Rilke, *Sonnets to Orpheus* 1.4, p. 9.

11. John Ashbery, *John Ashbery: Selected Poems* (London: Penguin, 1986), 221.

12. Ibid., 221.

13. Rilke, *Sonnets to Orpheus* 1.9, p.19.

14. Diana Ross and the Supremes, "Where Did Our Love Go," 1964.

15. *Les Fleurs du Mal* (1857) is the title of a series of autobiographical poems by Charles Baudelaire, an analytical study of the

boredom and apathy suffered by the overcultivated individual in the modern city.

16. The Pompidou Center in the Place Beaubourg, built 1974–76 and designed by Richard Rogers and Renzo Piano, is a modern art museum and cultural center of postmodern design. It is, as the poem indicates, a vast hangar-shaped building of glass and steel frame construction, ornamented with tubes and ducts and with a glass canister enclosing a moving staircase on the exterior.

17. Malin Pereira has drawn attention to *Mother Love* as being "much like T. S. Eliot's *The Waste Land,* a continuous parallel between the modern world and the world of myth." Pereira, *Rita Dove's Cosmopolitanism,* 142.

18. Malin Pereira reads this as a duet between mother and daughter. Ibid.

19. Quoted from *The Norton Anthology of African American Literature,* ed. Henry Louis Gates Jr. and Nellie Y. McKay (New York: W. W. Norton, 1997), 23.

20. Bellin, "Conversation with Rita Dove," 23 (Ingersoll, *Conversations,* 128).

21. Dove, "Intact World," xii.

22. Jan Heller Levi, ed., *A Muriel Rukeyser Reader* (New York: W. W. Norton, 1994), 213.

23. *Beloved* (London: Chatto and Windus, 1987), a novel set in the mid-nineteenth century, tells the story of Sethe, a southern slave who escapes to the North but, when threatened with recapture, murders her daughter to prevent her being sold into slavery. Later, her daughter, as Beloved, reappears, emblematic of all those lost, "disremembered and unaccounted for," asking for their story to be recovered. The novel closes with the ghostly traces of the missing daughter whose "footprints come and go, come and go" (274–75).

24. "*Ulysses,* Order and Myth" (1923), in *Selected Prose of T. S. Eliot,* ed. Frank Kermode (London: Faber, 1975), 177.

25. The figure of the urban saunterer, the sophisticated onlooker.

26. The phrase Henry James used about Americans (like himself) who spent a considerable time in Europe and acquired a cosmopolitan sensibility.

27. Lotta Lofgren in "Partial Horror: Fragmentation and Healing in Rita Dove's *Mother Love*," *Callaloo* 19, no. 1 (1996): 138, argues that *"Mother Love* is a psychomachy, illustrating the poet's own struggle with the disparate demands on mother, daughter, poet, and the imperfect yet sufficient truce between these warring roles."

28. Quoted from John J. L. Mood, "Rilke's Letters on Love," in *Rilke on Love and Other Difficulties: Translations and Considerations of Rainer Maria Rilke* (New York: Norton, 1975), 36.

29. Rilke, *Sonnets to Orpheus* 1.4, p. 9.

Chapter 7—*On the Bus with Rosa Parks*

Quotations from poems in Rita Dove's *On the Bus with Rosa Parks* are from the 1999 edition (New York: W. W. Norton).

1. "Autobiography," in Rita Dove, *Rita Dove: The Poet's World* (Washington, D.C.: Library of Congress, 1995), 85.

2. "Letter from Birmingham Jail" (1963), quoted from Gates and McKay, eds., *Norton Anthology of African American Literature,* 1865.

3. From "In the Lobby of the Warner Theatre, Washington, D.C.," in Dove, *On the Bus with Rosa Parks,* 86.

4. Bellin, "Conversation with Rita Dove," 19 (Ingersoll, *Conversations,* 127).

5. William Shakespeare, *The Tempest,* in *The Arden Shakespeare,* ed. Virginia Mason Vaughan and Alden T. Vaughan (Walton on Thames: Nelson, 1999), 5.1, p. 281.

6. This was premiered at Tanglewood with the Boston Symphony Orchestra on July 25, 1998.

7. Stevens, *Collected Poems,* 130.

8. This is the title of an article by Toni Morrison. See chapter 1, note 11.

9. Rilke, *Duino Elegies,* 25.

10. See Rilke's poem beginning "Oh this is the animal that never was," in Rilke, *Sonnets to Orpheus,* 63.

11. Bellin, "Conversation with Rita Dove," 27 (Ingersoll, *Conversations,* 131).

12. For explanations of *ekphrasis* and *ut pictura poesis,* see chapter 2, notes 8, 9, and 12.

13. Letter to George and Georgiana Keats, April 21, 1819, in *Selected Poems and Letters of Keats,* ed. Robert Gittings (1966; reprint, London: Heinemann), 118.

14. I attended Dove's reading on July 22, 1999 at Borders Bookshop, Oxford Street, London.

15. Brenda Shaughnessy, "Rita Dove: Taking the Heat," *Publishers Weekly,* April 12, 1999, 48.

16. Dove's reading, Borders Bookshop, July 22, 1999.

17. Mikhail Bakhtin, "Discourse in the Novel," 314–15.

18. Bishop, *Complete Poems,* 169.

19. This does not include Dove's *Selected Poems,* which comprises the first three volumes.

Chapter 8—Postscript

All quotations from Rita Dove's *American Smooth* are from the 2004 edition (New York: W. W. Norton).

1. Prefatory note, in Dove, *American Smooth,* n.p.

2. Emily Nussbaum, "Dance Fever," *New York Times Book Review* 109 (47): 9.

3. Rita Dove, "Notes," in Dove, *American Smooth,* 139.

4. In Lowell's poem "For the Union Dead," he refers to the Saint-Gaudens's bronze monument in Boston to Colonel Shaw, who commanded the first black regiment recruited in the North and died fighting for the Union during the Civil War. The regiment lost many men during a heroic assault on Fort Wagner in 1863. Lowell contrasts their bravery with the mercenary values and racist resistance to desegregation in the 1960s, declaring that the monument "sticks

like a fishbone / in the city's throat." *Robert Lowell: Collected Poems,* ed. Frank Bidart and David Gewanter (New York: Farrar, Strauss and Giroux, 2003), 377.

5. *Collected Poems: Robert Hayden,* ed. Frederick Glaysher (New York: Liveright, 1985), 51.

6. Noble Sissle's Swingsters were a celebrated New Orleans jazz band in the 1930s. Sissle was part of a gospel group in Indianapolis before the war. Barbeau and Henri record the incident that Dove uses in the poem in which Sissle went into the lobby of a hotel to buy a newspaper and was told by the manager to take off his hat. As, with change in one hand and newspaper in the other, he did not comply quickly enough, the manager "knocked off Sissle's hat, kicked him when he bent to pick it up, and kicked him again as he tried to leave." Arthur E. Barbeau and Florette Henri, *The Unknown Soldiers: Black American Troops in World War I* (Philadelphia: Temple University Press, 1974), 74.

7. Belleau Wood was tactically important because it was close to the Marne and within fifty miles of Paris. American Expeditionary Forces took heavy casualties in holding back the German advance, fighting in the confusing terrain of the forest. Dove has chosen to focus on one of the earlier engagements of 1917 rather than the later fighting between June 1 and 26 in 1918, for which the bravery of the American Marine Corps has become celebrated.

8. Barbeau and Henri recount that the Ninety-second Division, mostly draftees, was beset with difficulties including tensions within the command. The division was placed in an impossible situation during the September 1918 battles in the Argonne in which it failed to hold the Allied line and the black soldiers were accused of cowardice. See chapter 7 of Barbeau and Henri, *Unknown Soldiers,* for a detailed account.

9. "Well, I don't know what will happen now. We've got some difficult days ahead. But it doesn't matter with me now. Because I've been to the mountaintop. . . . And I've looked over. And I've seen the promised land." This was King's last sermon on civil rights, on April

3, 1968, the day before he was assassinated. Quoted from Gates and McKay, eds., *Norton Anthology of African American Literature,* 89.

10. Barbeau and Henri, *Unknown Soldiers,* has a photograph (illustration 19) of the 369th Infantry marching past the Flatiron Building in February 1919 in "the massed phalanx formation they had learned from the French." Barbeau and Henri quote from James Weldon Johnson, *Black Manhattan* (New York: Knopf, 1930), 235–36: "On the part of the men, there was no prancing, no showing of teeth, no swank; they marched with a steady stride; and from under their tin hats eyes that had looked straight at death were kept to the front." Barbeau and Henri, *Unknown Soldiers,* 174.

11. There are, in fact, thirteen poems in the volume, including one for the alternate juror who is not called to serve.

12. Renee H. Shea, "American Smooth: A Profile of Rita Dove," *Poets and Writers,* September/October 2004, 42.

Select Bibliography

Works by Rita Dove

Poetry

American Smooth. New York: W. W. Norton, 2004.

Grace Notes. New York: W. W. Norton, 1989.

Mother Love. New York: W. W. Norton, 1995.

Museum. Pittsburgh: Carnegie Mellon University Press, 1983.

On the Bus with Rosa Parks. New York: W. W. Norton, 1999.

Rita Dove: Selected Poems. New York: Vintage Books, 1993.

Thomas and Beulah. Pittsburgh: Carnegie Mellon University Press, 1986.

The Yellow House on the Corner. Pittsburgh: Carnegie Mellon University Press, 1980.

Fiction

Fifth Sunday. Short stories. Callaloo Fiction Series. Lexington: University of Kentucky Press, 1985.

Through the Ivory Gate. New York: Vintage, 1992.

Drama

The Darker Face of the Earth. Rev. 2nd ed. Brownsville, Tex.: Storyline Press, 1996.

Interviews

Ingersoll, Earl G., ed. *Conversations with Rita Dove*. Jackson: University Press of Mississippi, 2003.

Library of Congress Lectures

Rita Dove: The Poet's World. Washington, D.C.: Library of Congress, 1995.

Works about Rita Dove

Books and Chapters

Keller, Lynn. "Sequences Testifying for 'Nobodies': Rita Dove's *Thomas and Beulah* and Brenda Maria Osbey's *Desperate*

Circumstance, Dangerous Woman." In *Forms of Expansion: Recent Long Poems by Women,* chap. 3. Chicago: University of Chicago Press, 1997.

McDowell, Robert. "The Assembling Vision of Rita Dove." In *Conversant Essays: Contemporary Poets on Poetry,* edited by James McCorkle. Detroit: Wayne State University Press, 1990.

Pereira, Malin. *Rita Dove's Cosmopolitanism.* Urbana: University of Illinois Press, 2003.

Shoptaw, John. "Segregated Lives: Rita Dove's *Thomas and Beulah.*" In *Reading Black, Reading Feminist,* edited by Henry Louis Gates Jr. London: Penguin, 1990.

Steffen, Therese. *Crossing Color: Transcultural Space and Place in Rita Dove's Poetry, Fiction, and Drama.* Oxford: Oxford University Press, 2001.

Vendler, Helen. "The Black Dove: Rita Dove, Poet Laureate." In *Soul Says: On Recent Poetry.* Cambridge: Harvard University Press, 1995.

———. "A Dissonant Triad: Henri Cole, Rita Dove, and August Kleinzahler." In *Soul Says: On Recent Poetry.* Cambridge: Harvard University Press, 1995.

———. "Rita Dove: Identity Markers." In *The Given and the Made.* London: Faber, 1995.

Articles

Costello, Bonnie. "Scars and Wings: Rita Dove's *Grace Notes.*" *Callaloo* 14, no. 2 (1991): 434–38.

Cushman, Stephen. "And the Dove Returned." *Callaloo* 19, no. 1 (1996): 13–14.

Georgoudaki, Ekaterini. "Rita Dove: Crossing Boundaries." *Callaloo* 14, no. 2 (1991): 419–33.

Harrington, Walt. "The Shape of her Dreaming: Rita Dove Writes a Poem." *Washington Post Magazine,* May 7, 1995, 21–29.

Lofgren, Lotta. "Partial Horror: Fragmentation and Healing in Rita Dove's *Mother Love.*" *Callaloo* 19, no. 1 (1996): 135–42.

Rampersand, Arnold. "The Poems of Rita Dove." *Callaloo* 9, no. 1 (1986): 52–60.

Select Bibliography / 239

Wallace, Patricia. "Divided Loyalties: Literal and Literary in the Poetry of Lorna Dee Cervantes, Cathy Song, and Rita Dove." *Melus* 18 (Fall 1993): 3–19.

Interviews with Rita Dove

Interviews reprinted in Earl G. Ingersoll's *Conversations with Rita Dove* are indicated in parentheses as Ingersoll, *Conversations*.

Brazaltis, Tom. "Poet in Motion." *Plain Dealer,* February 26, 1995, 14.

Cavalieri, Grace. "Rita Dove: An Interview." *American Poetry Review* 24, no. 2 (March/April 1995): 10–15. (Ingersoll, *Conversations,* 136–47.)

Kirkpatrick, Patricia. "The Throne of Blues: An Interview with Rita Dove." *Hungry Mind Review* 35 (1995): 36–37.

Rubin, Stan Sanvel, and Judith Kitchen. "'The Underside of the Story': A Conversation with Rita Dove." In *The Post-Confessionals: Conversations with American Poets of the Eighties,* edited by Earl. G. Ingersoll, Judith Kitchen, and Stan Sanvel Rubin, 151–165. London: Associated University Presses 1989. (Ingersoll, *Conversations,* 3–14.)

Schneider, Steven. "Coming Home: An Interview with Rita Dove." *Iowa Review* 19, no. 3 (Fall 1989): 112–25. (Ingersoll, *Conversations,* 62–73.)

Shea, Renee H. "American Smooth: A Profile of Rita Dove." *Poets and Writers* 32, no. 5 (September/October 2004): 38–43.

Taleb-Khyar, Mohamed B. "An Interview with Maryse Condé and Rita Dove." *Callaloo* 14, no. 2 (1991): 347–66. (Ingersoll, *Conversations,* 74–87.)

Vendler, Helen. "An Interview with Rita Dove." In *Reading Black, Reading Feminist,* edited by Henry Louis Gates Jr., 481–91. London: Penguin, 1990.

Walsh, William. "Isn't Reality Magic? An Interview with Rita Dove." *Kenyon Review* 16, no. 3 (1994): 142–54.

Index